Glory Land

To Greg Morris —
God bless you!

Jym Cydem

See you later!

Glory Land

A Memoir of a Lifetime in Church

Lyn Cryderman

ZondervanPublishingHouse
Grand Rapids, Michigan

A Division of HarperCollinsPublishers

Glory Land

Copyright © 1999 by Lyn Cryderman

Requests for information should be addressed to:

 ZondervanPublishingHouse

Grand Rapids, Michigan 49530

Library of Congress Cataloging-in-Publication Data

Cryderman, Lyn.

Glory land : a memoir of a lifetime in church / Lyn Cryderman.

    p.   cm.

ISBN 0-310-22454-3 (hardcover)

1. Cryderman, Lyn.   2. Free Methodist Church of North America—United States—Clergy—Biography.   I. Title.

BX8495.C78A3 1999

287' .2'092—dc21   99-10104

                                                   CIP

This edition printed on acid-free paper and meets the American National Standards Institute Z39.48 standard.

Cover photo of the author by W. Dale Cryderman

Printed in the United States of America

99 00 01 02 03 04 05 /❖ DC/ 10 9 8 7 6 5 4 3 2 1

To Esther and her children:
Jesse. Emma. Molly. Eli. My best friends.

Acknowledgments

*C*redit *for so much of what is in this book belongs to the parents God* gave me, Dale and Dorothy Cryderman. They and my brothers—Bill, Dale, and Rik—are responsible for most of the good that is in my life. No single event has had as profound effect on my spiritual nurture than my father's decision to cart us all off to Japan as missionaries and then bring us back home in the manner described in this book.

The better part of my "lifetime in church" occurred in a small denomination known as the Free Methodist Church, and I am grateful to the hundreds of dear saints in that family whose lives provided so much material for this book.

My publisher, Scott Bolinder, also happens to be my boss and friend, and the fact that he remains both after publishing this book says more about him than about me. Stan Gundry, editorial vice president, inspired me with his own stories of growing up in a parsonage. My editor, Sandy Vander Zicht, and her teammate, Bob Hudson, are so good it's scary.

In every publishing company, there are scores of people who bring a book to life. People like Jean Bloom who have to keep everyone on schedule, and Stine May, Sue Johnson, and Ann Schrouder who know all my bad habits and are still nice to me. Joyce Ondersma's job, along with help from Jackie Aldridge and

Suzie Boeckel, is to keep authors happy. I am happy! John Topliff, Emily Klotz, Greg Stielstra, and Dr. Hooks made sure you knew about this book, and Jeff Ray made sure his sales reps sold it. Zondervan's award-winning distribution center, led by people like Al Kerkstra, Bud Zondervan (the answer is yes), Paul MacDonald, and Cathy Schut practically handed this book to you, so good is their service.

Finally, I have been blessed with many friends who seldom go to church and have therefore made me aware of both the strangeness and wonder of a lifetime in church. I could not have written this book without their friendship, and my prayer is that something in this book will ignite a desire to give church a try.

Contents

❧

11
INTRODUCTION:
Do You Remember the Motions?

17
ONE—Old Enough to Know

23
TWO—Sanctuary

33
THREE—To Preach the Gospel

43
FOUR—Just Passing Through

53
FIVE—A Church to Call Home

65
SIX—Opening Exercises

79
SEVEN—Lover's Lane

93
EIGHT—Church in the Woods

103
NINE—Revival Fire

117
TEN—Winning Souls

131
ELEVEN—Unanswered Prayers

151
TWELVE—Lost and Found

161
THIRTEEN—Discovering Church . . . Again

169
FOURTEEN—Glory Land

Introduction

Do You Remember the Motions?

*"There's a fountain flowing
deep and wide."*

⌒

I have spent most of my life in church.

For the first sixteen or so years, I had no choice. My daddy was either the pastor, or we were missionaries. But in the 1950s and '60s, it really didn't matter because it seemed as if most everyone went to church. In the small town where my family eventually settled—a languid village blessed with just one church, one grocery store, and one traffic light—you either went to church on Sunday morning, Sunday night, Wednesday night, and the whole week when a revival came to town, or you were a pagan.

There were few pagans in Spring Arbor, Michigan, in the '50s and '60s.

I cannot say I always wanted to be in church each Sunday for more than two hours in the morning, and then back again in the evening for yet another hour-and-a-half of singing, praying, and listening to a sermon. In fact, I dreaded waking up to hearing the sound of Bill Pierce and Dick Anthony on the hi-fi because it signaled that this was not Saturday, a day meant for baseball and catching snakes in the swamp, or even a school day, which was almost as bad as Sunday, but not quite. This was the Lord's Day, and if I thought the hi-fi was a false alarm, the hissing of the pressure cooker and aroma of pot roast confirmed my worst fears. Another perfectly good day was about to be ruined.

I'm sure I protested then as my own children do now, though to tell you the truth I really don't remember many discussions about whether or not church would become that Sunday morning's venue of choice. Looking back, it seemed out of the question to question going to church. I *do* remember feigning illness—even so far as to hold the thermometer close to the lamp beside my bed—in order to be allowed to stay home, but that almost always backfired later in the day. "If you were sick enough to miss church, you're too sick to go outside and play." Moot point, for what constituted play on a Sunday in our home was fairly narrowly defined in those days. I think the main reason why I do not enjoy board games, naps, or taking walks is because that was all I could do for "play" on a Sunday. No bike riding. No sports. No television.

Can you imagine Sunday afternoon without television?

You would think that being forced to go to church and then having to come home to a walk, a nap, or a game of *Sorry* would turn me away from Sunday services for good. It did not. True enough, I rebelled, which for me meant skipping church whenever I felt like it while I was in college. But once I got married, I found myself drawn back to the pew. It did not hurt that I married a Baptist girl who not only spent more time in church as a youngster than I did, but won every sword drill to boot. (If you do not know what a sword drill is, I can guess your age or former church affiliation.) To this day, when our pastor announces the text for his sermon, she's on her Bible like a cat, flipping pages until she gives me that raised-eyebrow glance that says, "What took you so long?"

Forced church attendance may not have been politically or biblically correct, but who cared in 1958? Besides, it did not seem to hurt either of us. At least not too much. I am almost ashamed to admit how many times on a Saturday night I have pretty much decided I'd "let the kids sleep in" the next morning, or how many times I would wake up on that next morning and be tempted to grab the Sunday paper and a thermos of coffee for a leisurely morning on the front porch. On the other hand, I have a sort of smug pride in knowing that most of the time I shrugged off those seductions and led the troops out the door and off to Sunday school. So for the past twenty-eight years of married life, even though no one was keeping score, on most any given Sunday you would find me in Sunday school, then church, and until recently, heading back for the evening service (for some reason the church we now attend set the time of their Sunday evening service at 5:00; who wants to shut the game off in the middle of the second half?).

It may be true that my preacher's-kid pedigree makes my personal church history unique, though my hunch is that I'm not the only Baby Boomer who spent a lot of time in church. Despite a lot of new growth in evangelical churches, the vast majority of adults who are now in church nearly every Sunday can point to a long and sometimes glorious record of church *association* if not actual attendance. If you don't quite believe me, try this little experiment the next time you head out of your aisle on a Sunday morning. First introduce yourself to your worship neighbors and then ask them when they started going to church. When I do this, almost always the "lifers" exceed the number of brand-new-to-the-faith attenders by about three or four to one. George Barna I'm not, of course, but even *his* numbers are pretty impressive. Of the ninety-two to ninety-eight million born-again

Christians in America, he says that at least sixty-four percent started attending church as youngsters. True, they may have gone AWOL for a period—usually from about age eighteen until their first child is about four—but Sunday school is very much a part of a Boomer's past. Maybe that's why you can hum or whistle "Jesus Loves Me" in a crowded airport terminal and someone is sure to recognize it.

There are a lot more of us around than we think.

I have written this book for all of us who have spent a lifetime in Sunday school; for everyone who remembers all the words to "Climb, Climb Up Sunshine Mountain" and can still remember the smell of white paste and crayons and damp church basement Sunday school rooms. I believe our years of memorizing Scripture and sitting through object lessons and bringing a friend so that we both won a pencil were a great treasure that needs to be savored and somehow preserved. I wrote this book for the true believer who may not actually want to do songs with "motions" anymore but realizes there is something missing in his or her journey of faith that might benefit from at least a good chorus or two of "Do Lord."

I am thankful that the church has become more sophisticated and that my kids can play basketball on Sunday. I do not much mind praise choruses on video walls in theater-like "worship centers," and I must admit that padded seats are a lot more comfortable than wooden pews. Maybe this is a middle-age thing, but while I enjoy so much of what church means to me today, I want to hold on to something of what it was yesterday. And although I'm pretty certain your kids will never get too excited about playing *Sorry* on Sunday, I hope that through this book you also will find ways to re-create for them the spiritual nurture and care—unvarnished, uncool, and even a bit uncomfortable—that you were given in your youth.

If you are any kind of a Sunday school veteran, you will soon recognize that each chapter begins with a line from some of those songs we used to sing as the "Sunday school superintendent" warmed us up for the trek down to the classrooms in the church basement. Just for fun, I walked into a meeting at work the other day humming one of those tunes. Sure enough, someone else joined in, but he added the words. What surprised me was that since my duet partner was quite a bit younger than I, he should have been more of a praise chorus kind of guy. Curious, I asked him where he learned that song. "Vacation Bible School!" he answered, then he added, "Yeah, Dominic, my five-year-old, came home singing that and was so proud he knew all the motions." Three generations of us separated by time and denomination, yet we still knew how to march in the infantry because there we were, all "in the Lord's army." There is hope, I thought, as I gunned down the Enemy with my imaginary artillery.

Someday, Dominic will be my age, and I will be an old man. Because his father takes him to Sunday school, chances are good that he will carry our faith throughout his life. We may even cross paths. If we do, I will ask Dominic, "Do you still know all the motions? Have you taught them to your sons and daughters?"

Maybe then we will both sing that silly little song together, a very old man and a middle-aged father. If we do, I hope there will still be younger men and boys and girls who will hear us and for a moment forget who they are and where they are and join us.

And I hope right now a flood of sights and sounds from Sunday schools past are surging through your soul as we begin a journey back into the nursery of our faith.

LYN CRYDERMAN

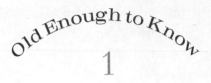

1

"Little ones to him belong."

cro

*W*hat woke me up first were the footsteps.

Listen.

You are in the first house of your memory. You had been tucked in gently with prayers and fell asleep on the arms of innocent dreams. You stir, roll into a tighter fetal tuck, and as you turn from the wall you squint at the small ray of light coming from beneath the door. You know from the shoes on the hardwood floor when the whole house was supposed to be asleep that something was wrong. And then the voices. Mostly your mamma, with a word or two from your daddy. They are talking quietly so as not to wake you up, which makes you strain to listen until you are fully alert. Daddy must be going somewhere. It has happened before, but it always makes you nervous. He is a preacher, and if someone dies in the night or their kid has not come home, they call Daddy and he goes. That's his job.

Then I heard the squealing and what sounded like a huge truck that had got stuck and was spinning its wheels trying to get going again. The wind rattled the window panes, and it was raining hard.

Normally lightning did not scare me, but I jumped when it lit up my room, instantly followed by a sharp blast of thunder. I heard Daddy walk down the stairway that led to the first floor of the parsonage. To the right was the living room with a large fireplace and windows that looked out over Chestnut Street. The dining room and kitchen lay to the left. There was a huge white electric stove with a deep cylinder next to one of the burners where you could slip in a kettle for making soup. But Daddy was heading out the front door, which was at the end of a little foyer directly in front of the banister-lined staircase. The squealing continued, and I heard men's voices hollering outside my window which faced Ninth Avenue. Pretty soon Mamma slipped into my room and knelt next to the bed, her soft, cool hand reaching for my forehead like she did when she checked to see if I had a fever.

"I'm scared, Mamma."

She told me that a train had slipped off its tracks and that an "animal car" filled with pigs had tipped over. That was what the squealing was. I asked her if the pigs would be okay and she said that she thought so, but the noise they made sounded like they were hurt real bad.

"Are they gonna die?" I asked.

"Oh, I think they'll be okay. They're just scared."

The room was dark except for a thin stream of light spilling in from my parents' bedroom at the end of the hall and the occasional lightning flash that turned everything white for an instant. Outside, the wind came now in gusts that whistled through the giant walnut trees, throwing sheets of rain against the window.

"If they die, will they go to heaven?"

My mamma did not go to college or seminary, but I never knew her to sidestep a tough question. She had been the valedictorian of her class at Mesick High School, a tiny railroad town in northern

Michigan along the banks of the Manistee River. Mushroom capitol of the world, according to the sign out by the county landfill. She met my daddy there, after his own daddy died of tuberculosis, the same disease that struck my daddy as a boy and left him crippled. When the boys played baseball out behind the school, a buddy held Daddy's crutches as he stood in the batter's box, then tossed them to him when he hit the ball. A single was about all he could get out of a home run.

They got married right after they graduated, and headed downstate to Detroit, Daddy's hometown. He got a job as a news photographer for the *Detroit Times*, and even though they both grew up in the church—Daddy was a preacher's kid too—the pull of the newsroom was too much for Daddy. When he wasn't working on a Sunday, they headed for Belle Isle to watch the boats steam up and down the Detroit River. Church sort of drifted out of their lives.

Daddy had a nose for news. In addition to covering the Tigers in Briggs Stadium and Joe "the Brown Bomber" Louis, he seemed to always know where the mob bosses hung out and took delight in photographing them. Once, when a young member of "the Purple Gang" was sitting in the holding pen at a local precinct, Daddy pulled up his camera for a mug shot.

"Hey buddy, my old man's dying of cancer and it'll kill him to see me like this." He had his hands over his face, so Daddy told him to relax. He wouldn't take the picture. As soon as the guy's arms go down, Daddy shoots. The guy grabs an ink well and throws it at Daddy, but he's already out the door to meet a deadline.

In those days, the photographers had to develop their own film. After finishing up in the lab, they would have a few drinks and then start with the tricks. One of his favorites was taking the giant wads of wet cotton used to wipe off the negatives, open a window on the seventeenth floor of the building, and drop them on unsuspecting pedestrians below.

Loren and Francis Bradley, a married couple about their age who attended the church my grandpa pastored before he died, would stop by my parents' house now and then and invite them to church, but Daddy wasn't interested. He does not talk about this much, but when their first child, Billy, was born, Daddy went on a bender. He booked a hotel room and invited his newsroom buddies to a party that lasted two days and two nights.

Loren was a tool and die man. Not much for words. But he had a heart for God and remembered when Dale Cryderman did too. When Daddy came down with a strange illness that put him flat on his back, Loren stopped by his house on Buchanan Street and over coffee he and Daddy engaged in the kind of small talk that men engage in to keep from talking about more important things. The most important thing on both their minds was the word from the doctor earlier in the week that Daddy's illness was life threatening. Just before he got up to leave, and with a fair amount of awkwardness, Loren grabbed Daddy's hand and said, "Fella, I'm prayin' for ya'." It broke Daddy's heart, softening his resolve a little to keep God out of his life, but not enough to make him surrender.

But the next day, probably on a tip from Loren, a Sunday school teacher from church stopped by for a visit and got right to the point. Looking him square in the eye, he said, "Dale, you could be saved tonight." That was all it took. With my mamma kneeling by his side, both of them returned to the fold on January 18, 1939.

Daddy promised God that if he could beat the illness he would step through any open door and serve him the rest of his life. God kept his end of the deal. Daddy got a clean bill of health from his doctor the next day. He went back to the newsroom and told his buddies that he had got saved and that he was going to become a preacher. His old drinking buddies promptly gave him a nickname: Deacon. Within a few months Dale Cryderman traded his Speed Graphic for a Bible and has been preaching ever since.

I had heard his sermons practically from the day I was born, but as the storm settled in on Winona Lake, Indiana, that night and the pigs shrieked in the darkness, for the first time in my life I thought about my own self dying and started crying. Mamma had been humming "If I Gained the World but Lost the Savior," a song she often sang during the day as she did the laundry, but when she heard me sob, she asked me what was wrong.

"I don't wanna die, Mamma."

She pulled me closer and gently assured me that I wouldn't die real soon but that if I had Jesus in my heart I didn't need to worry about dying because I would go to heaven.

"Do you have Jesus in your heart?" she asked.

"I think so."

Mamma told me all I had to do was ask, and then she prayed with me just to make sure.

I was three years old.

Sanctuary

2

"Leaning on the everlasting arms."

∽

I can describe nearly every room in that parsonage—how it was actually connected to the church and how you could enter the side balcony of the sanctuary from a hallway where my daddy had his darkroom. He might have left the newsroom, but he couldn't resist grabbing a camera when the fire siren sounded, hollering for us to get in the car. It might be two in the morning, but we would jump into our clothes and stumble down the stairs and into the car even as it was pulling out of the garage. The trick was to see which direction the fire truck headed and then chase it down in a sort of perverse anticipation. I mean, no one really wanted to see a family lose all its belongings, but then again, it would be a shame to go to all that trouble for nothing. Most of the time it was nothing—maybe someone left the oven on with something in it, or a half-burnt leaf pile flared up in the night. But about once a year it would be the real thing, and Daddy would snap pictures of the firemen trying to save the house, then rush home to develop them so that he could drop them off at the local newspaper before it went to press.

I can tell you the exact location where the basketball rim was attached to a telephone pole in the backyard and where the pipe for the oilman to deliver heating oil poked up out of the ground because I remember getting punished for plugging it up with green walnuts.

I can describe the steeple where my oldest brother, Bill, and my daddy crawled up one night to install a small television antenna so as not to get caught by any church members. Bill was wedged into the steeple with Daddy, and it was his job to holler down to my next oldest brother, Dale, who was leaning out the window of the room where we had the television set. Daddy would point the antenna toward Ft. Wayne or South Bend (depending on which channel they wanted to watch) while Bill would listen to Dale reporting on the reception. The rest of us sat quietly as we watched the screen—which was shaped like a ship's porthole—yield images that faded in and out of a grey-and-white pattern of dots. When we could actually see humanlike shapes, Dale would yell up to Bill who would tell Daddy to hold it right there, which, because of the reaction time, allowed the antenna to move a few degrees off target. After five or six tries, Daddy locked it into place and declared it as good as it was going to get.

We watched Mr. Wizard, George Burns and Gracie Allen, and the Friday night fights sponsored by Gillette, but if a cigarette or beer commercial came on, we had to turn our heads while Daddy turned off the volume. Still, because of television, I can tell you that Lucky Strike means fine tobacco, that Winston tastes good like a (clap, clap) cigarette should, and that Blatz is Milwaukee's favorite beer. Which was probably why the trustees didn't want a television in the parsonage.

I can describe the National radio with a metal exterior tuning dial that sat beside my daddy's side of the bed and stayed on all night long because he loved to hear someone talking whenever he couldn't sleep, which was often. Even though his leg brace came off shortly after he was married, he never experienced a minute without pain. Ever. When the local radio station, WRSW, signed off at midnight, he would alternate between KMOX in St. Louis and WGN in Chicago. Maybe because of that, there are few sounds that are as soothing to me as that of a man's voice floating through static and a speaker grill, illuminated by the dim light of a radio dial.

I can draw a detailed picture of my "Blue Buick," a pedal car that I would drive round and round the folding chairs in the youth group's basement Sunday school room while my brother Dale played gospel tunes from the spiral-bound red, white, and blue Singspiration chorus book. The faster he would play, the faster I would pedal.

Even though they have since been demolished, I can take you to the exact location of the Eskimo Inn, Billy Sunday Tabernacle, and the Lakeside Roller Rink, the major tourist attractions in our little village. Every summer, the town of Winona Lake became a major stagecoach stop on the sawdust trail. Organizations like Youth for Christ, Moody Bible Institute (believe it or not, their event was called Moody Week), Oriental Missionary Society, the Christian Holiness Association, the Fellowship of Christian Magicians, and several denominations invaded for a week of meetings that would fill the huge tabernacle named after the baseball player-turned evangelist. Set into the hill behind the tabernacle were boarding houses with names like "Haven of Rest," and "Still Waters," where entire families would crowd into a single room for the week just so they could go to the preaching services three times a day. In between services, they would line up at the Eskimo Inn for a trayfull of macaroni and cheese and a cup of coffee. Most weeks the teenagers would head for the roller rink at night or opt for a cruise around the lake on the *Winona Queen,* an old paddle-wheeler docked behind the roller rink. I would venture to guess that of the hundreds of evangelical ministries that have been around since the turn of the century, you would be hard pressed to find many of their leaders who did not spend a week in Winona Lake at some point in their lives.

I can show you the dock where my brother Bill launched a motorboat he had built and then watched it sink to the bottom of the lake before he ever had a chance to take it for a spin. It was a rough year for Bill. A few months later he crashed through the offensive line to block a punt for the mighty Warsaw Tigers, his high school football team. In those days they wore helmets without protective face masks. So instead of diving right into the kicker, as most football players would do today, he turned at the last minute and took the full force of the boot in the seat of his pants, resulting in an inglorious sports injury if there ever was one. The doctor called it a broken pelvis, but his friends laughed that he broke his butt. In fairness to Bill, we have all had our share of ignominy, owing largely to the example set by our father. You learn something about your genetic shortcomings when you see your daddy sail over the handlebars of a wheelbarrow or look up at the last second to see the axe-head that slipped from his grasp land squarely on his forehead. Such disasters were the norm among the men of our household.

I can direct you to the dirt race track in New Paris where my daddy spent many Saturday nights, not only because he enjoyed the stock car races, but because he was trying to get close to Joe Cutler, an unsaved father of one of his Sunday school kids, Joe Jr. I'm not sure who ended up happier—Joe, for getting Jesus in his heart, or Daddy, for getting a chance to take Joe's car out on the track for a few hot laps. I have heard my daddy use this story to encourage young preachers to be willing to do things they don't like in order to get close to those who need the Lord. But if you had seen my daddy's face as he powered that car around the track, you would have thought that he didn't much mind being used of God in such a manner.

I can walk you across the street from the parsonage to the old Westminster Hotel and into a room where legend has it that Billy Graham once prayed with a group of men before his first crusade in Los Angeles, receiving confirmation from the Lord that he was being called to be an evangelist. I have not been able to confirm this, which is not unusual. My daddy says that dozens of people have come up to him over the years and claimed they were present at the service where he got saved despite the fact that he never got saved at a public service. Inspiration among the church folk who raised me was not always dependent on accuracy.

Finally, I can take you into every office and room of the Publishing House, just up the street from the parsonage, and introduce you to the memories of Lloyd Knox and Rosie McClung and Charles Kingsley and John Benson and Dan Howard and John McClements and Charles Kirkpatrick and Myron Boyd. The Publishing House is one of my favorite places in the whole world. Even though everyone called it "the Publishing House," it was also the headquarters of the Free Methodist Church of North America, the denomination I was born into. Since not many people have heard of this group, I will share a story about one of our bishops who was addressing a group of the *other* Methodists.

"You may wonder what Free Methodists are," he said at the beginning of his address to a roomful of United Methodists. "Well, we are about as free as you are united."

When you walked through the front door of the Publishing House, the smell of ink and paper made everything seem full of importance, as did the wide, lacquered staircase leading upstairs to where the bishops had their offices. Surrounding a wide hallway on the main floor were the offices of denominational executives in charge of missions and evangelism and education, as well as youth and the Women's Missionary Society. Next to the ornamental staircase was a small door leading to a narrow stairway winding down into the basement where all the typesetting and printing took place.

Most of the people who worked there attended my daddy's church, so just by walking through and saying hello he kept in touch with a fair percentage of his parishioners. If I was lucky, he took me with him, which always meant I would leave with a pencil or an eraser or a piece of chewing gum from one of the secretaries.

Since the Publishing House, surrounded by acres of rolling landscape, was right across the street from the parsonage, I spent a lot of time exploring the grounds with my Sunday school friend, Johnny Siefken. The three-story brick building stood at the end of a U-shaped drive guarded by maple-tree sentries created by God himself for climbing—if you could get up into the branches before one of the secretaries saw you and reported you to a janitor who could make you come down just by telling you to.

In those days, every adult was your parent.

You could walk into a drug store and stand looking at the candy counter and within thirty seconds the clerk would tell you that you weren't suppose to have candy until Saturday. The clerk knew that because she lived in the same town as you did and went to Women's Missionary Society meetings with your mamma where, in addition to rolling bandages for Kibogora Hospital somewhere in Africa, they talked about their kids. "Dorothy, it tickles me pink every time Lyn comes in asking for candy." "Don't give him any, Margaret. He can only have candy on Saturdays, and then only if he's been good all week."

You could have sneaked down the hill to the lake to catch frogs and someone would appear out of nowhere and tell you that you weren't supposed to be near the water without your older brother. A kid drowned once in that lake sometime not too long ago— could have been fifty years ago—so now every adult keeps watch for any little kid near the lake without a big kid nearby.

In church it was worse because your daddy was the preacher and so adults not only had to cope with their own natural inclination to raise every kid in the neighborhood, but they also wanted to make sure your daddy knew they were watching out for you because, after all, you were the preacher's kid. So if, for example, you went up to the balcony before church started, "I don't think your daddy wants you up here" greeted you like a voice from heaven, though it was only the guy who ran the sound system, which in those days was a DuKane amplifier and a ribbon mike. If you passed a note behind your mamma's back to your little brother during a hymn, a wrinkled hand clutching a hankie would intercept it and hand it over to your mamma and then she would smile at you like she was so grateful for the chance to help Mamma handle you in church, which was no small task.

Four of us, all boys, gave folks plenty of opportunity to help mamma out. Sometimes, however, all the help in the world wasn't enough to keep us in line, and it seemed as if those occasions always happened in church. I will never forget my daddy stopping in the middle of a sermon and looking not at Mamma but at each of us boys, back and forth and back and forth and saying, "Dorothy, if you don't make those boys behave, I'm coming down there and doing it myself," which would have suited us just fine because in front of witnesses he would have been much easier on us than he was about an hour later back at the parsonage.

To this day, I cannot run in church. I now have no reason to, of course, but even if the occasion demanded it—let's say a fire alarm went off or I saw someone about to steal my car in the parking lot or the place was empty and a carnal urge to run swept over me—I would not be *able* to run for fear of someone appearing from around the corner or stepping out of the ladies room right at that moment just to say in a loud whisper, "We don't *run* in God's house."

I cannot read from a Sunday school paper in church today, partly because we do not *have* Sunday school papers anymore but also because I am certain a hand will reach over my shoulder and firmly but quietly close the paper to remind me that we also do not read in church, excepting the Bible, of course, but preferably only those passages mentioned by the preacher, which you can bet would never include the Song of Solomon. Have you ever wondered how we *found* those verses since no one ever preached on them or asked us to memorize them?

I cannot do a lot of things in and out of church because the village that raised me took its job seriously, even at the risk of being forever thought of as busybodies.

But Lyle Martin was not like that. Lyle shipped Sunday school papers from the basement of the Publishing House, and I don't ever recall him telling us kids not to do anything, which is not to say he was less religious than those dear saints who helped my mamma raise me. To tell the truth, he always seemed to me like the most religious man I knew. For one thing, he had the whitest hair I had ever seen, then or now, and white hair to me will always belong to the wisest and most spiritual men in any congregation. That, plus the fact that he arrived at church before anyone else, and that he smiled so much that he looked friendly even when he wasn't smiling, was enough for me to think of him as maybe the best Christian in the whole church, except for my daddy who didn't really count because he *had* to be the best Christian.

In the hierarchy of church life in our parents' generation, Lyle knew his place. On the upstairs floors in windowed offices were bishops and evangelists who traveled all over this world preaching the gospel and raising money. They wore suits and always smelled of Vitalis and Old Spice, and had secretaries who were mostly middle-aged and mostly single. Their admiration for their bosses was akin to a nun's regard for the Pope, and you can imagine what that would do to your ego if you were one of the men upstairs.

Lyle's job kept him in the basement, which was where the guts of the publishing business was. I think his official calling was distribution, but Lyle was the kind of guy who could repair one of the German printing presses or sharpen the cutting machine's swordlike blade, and if the men's room hadn't been cleaned that day, he would scrub it down himself and not complain. When my daddy would announce from the pulpit that a few men were needed to rake the church lawn or freshen up the building with a coat of paint, Lyle was always the first man on the scene. I don't recall seeing anyone from upstairs show up.

It would be wrong and dangerous to say that Lyle really was a better Christian than the men upstairs—better than all of us—but when it came to the things that seem to matter most to God, he stood above the crowd. For all the Lyles we remember, you could read the blessed Beatitudes and say at the end of each, "That's him!" Every church had one, or, if they were really lucky, had several. What made them so attractive to us was that despite their status in the Kingdom, they did not think they were special, nor did they aspire to go upstairs. I cannot be certain, but I think it was men and women like Lyle whom the Bible was talking about when it said the last will become first.

There was another reason why I thought Lyle Martin must have been about as close to God as you could get. After the benediction and *Doxology*, when we kids had had about as much sitting as a kid could take and the scratchiness of our collars made us almost crazy, we slipped out of our mamma's grip and tried to snake through the forest of wool and linen and nylon, only to be grabbed by a surrogate mamma and told to slow down. We would walk politely just long enough to get outside her reach, then dash on out through the foyer and sneak under arms reaching for my daddy's handshake at the door, burst into the sunlight, and make a quick right turn.

He was always there.

Arms outstretched and standing about three feet below, just to the side of the wrought-iron railing alongside the steps next to one of the giant white columns that held up the roof. One by one we would take our turns, jumping into those strong arms without the slightest fear that he would drop us, and liking it so much we would fight traffic back up the stairs and jump again.

We were too young to realize that we were jumping into the arms of God; learning—as no sermon could preach—about faith and trust and security. In fact, most of what I learned about God came from the hands and arms and feet of the church people who helped my parents raise me.

I could not have known that every hand that closed a Sunday school paper during the sermon or slowed me when I was running in the sanctuary or intercepted a game of hangman was a lesson about the church. Those arms and hands and feet were body parts without which I would have wandered farther from the fold than I actually did in later years. They represented real people whose flaws never overshadowed their hearts' desire to shepherd another child into the kingdom of God.

What a fellowship. What a joy divine.

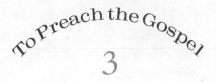

To Preach the Gospel

3

"There are souls to rescue,
there are souls to save."

ↄ

I don't remember my daddy telling us we were going to be missionaries, but I do remember packing the 1952 Ford Ranch Wagon in front of the parsonage. Daddy was going to drive it from Winona Lake, Indiana, to San Francisco, where it would be put inside the same ship that would sail us to Japan.

While my older brothers loaded up the real luggage, I slipped something in that seemed important to me at the time: a handful of leaves. I am not sure why I did this, but I remember being very serious about collecting just the right ones from beneath the trees that shaded our yard and then carefully placing them just inside the tailgate on the left hand side of the car. Funny what you remember, isn't it?

When I asked my daddy why we were going to Japan, he said it was to preach the gospel. He had recently returned from a six-week trip to the Orient, ostensibly as a United Nations war correspondent in Korea, but I think that was just his way of making sure he could get up to the front lines to try and find Joe Cutler Jr., the race-car driver's son, one of Daddy's Sunday school boys who was now a grunt in the army.

In my daddy's newspaper days, he once covered seven murders in five days. What he had seen and recorded with notebook and camera in Korea, however, touched him in that spot in one's heart that cannot be protected by the cold objectivity of journalism. He traveled all over Korea with a great bear of a man named Bob Pierce who was trying to do something for the thousands of children orphaned by the war, something that eventually came to be called World Vision.

When he got back, Daddy would talk about the war in some of his sermons, reporting on "our boys" who were freezing to death in the Korean hills. But when he talked about the Korean refugees who had escaped from the communist north or the young prisoners he visited in Japan's reform schools, he would stumble with emotion, compose himself, and continue in a broken voice about how they did not know Jesus.

Like me, he grew up in a culture where everyone had at least heard of Jesus and most believed in Him. It was incomprehensible to my daddy that you could visit the temple grounds in Tokyo and see thousands of people bow down to Buddha and not have the slightest knowledge of our Savior. He could not go back and preach in a church where everyone knew Jesus. It was almost blasphemous to him. Why bring the Good News to people who already had it? So that was why we were going to Japan, and because I loved my daddy and trusted his Jesus, I had a ready answer when anyone asked about our upcoming trip: "I'm going to Japan to preach the gospel."

It turned out that I was telling the truth, because it was not long before my daddy realized that a blonde, light-skinned child was a big draw at the street rallies he conducted to preach the gospel. The year was 1952, a heady time to be a missionary in Japan. They had just lost a war, their economy was in a mess, and along comes a family from the very country they once feared and hated. We worked alongside Jake De Shazer, one of the bombardiers on the mission that dropped the atomic bomb on Hiroshima and Nagasaki. His plane got hit as it lumbered back to the aircraft carrier, and Jake and his crew had to parachute into the hands of the enemy. In prison, he made one of those dangerous bargains with God: he promised to preach the gospel the rest of his life if he got out alive. Two of his captured buddies died; three others were executed. Jake got out on after forty months and promptly returned to love his enemies.

Jake would visit our home and put me on his knee and ask me why I was in Japan and then roll his head back and laugh when I answered, "To preach the gospel."

The Japanese paid attention when we set up the flatbed semi-trailer with loudspeakers, microphones, lights, and musical instruments. Who wouldn't? Imagine a major intersection in one of the largest cities in the world. Three or four white-gloved policeman stop traffic so the semi can back the trailer into place. Volunteers appear out of the throng of pedestrians and readily agree to pass out little folded sheets of paper telling about a Jesus they had never heard of. (My daddy told me he thinks I personally handed out more than a million tracts during one rally alone in Tokyo that was dubbed "Operation Saturation.") As night falls, the colored lights flood the trailer and the loudspeakers come alive with music. My older brothers take their positions—Dale on the guitar, Bill at the accordion. Nambu-san, a tall, gregarious Japanese Christian, tips his trombone toward the stars, and Jingo-san sings. I cannot understand the words, but I know them from the tune:

Would you be free from your burden of sin,
There's power in the blood, power in the blood.
Would you o'er evil a victory win,
There's wonderful power in the blood.

I do not know how this song translated into Japanese, but I suspect however it came out it violated all we now know about delivering the precious gospel in a context acceptable to the hearer. We did not stop to think what these people who saw so much bloodshed would think when they saw their enemies singing about blood and victory over evil. It didn't seem to matter, because the more we sang, the larger the crowd grew.

> What a friend we have in Jesus,
>> All our sins and grief to bear.
> What a privilege to carry,
>> Everything to God in prayer.

My little brother, Rik, and I dressed up in kimonos and wooden shoes called *ghetta* and sang that one in Japanese. Today, I remember just enough of it to make my children fall over laughing when I sing it: *"Itsu kuki me foo cocky."* In Tokyo in 1952 it just packed them in tighter as passersby strained to see the two little American boys wearing Japanese clothes and singing in their language. Talk about making them ripe for the picking. We used the formula that a then-young evangelist named Billy Graham employed so successfully stateside: lively music, celebrity testimony, and then a gospel sermon, straight from the Bible. By the time Jake De Shazer told how he had Nagasaki in his bomb sights and then was shot down and captured and thrown into a prison where he met Jesus who told him to return to Japan and love his enemies, about the only sound you could hear was the distant rumble of a subway passing a few blocks away.

Then Daddy would preach.

I have forgotten the stories, but I'll always remember the Scriptures:

"For all have sinned and come short of the glory of God."

"The wages of sin is death."

"If we confess our sin he is faithful and just to forgive us our sin."

"For God so loved the world that he gave his only begotten son."

"Behold I stand at the door and knock."

When my brother Bill started playing "Just As I Am" on his accordion, it was harvest time in Tokyo. Whether they came out of curiosity or conviction, we may never know, and I will leave it to the theologians to decide whether or not a simple prayer of confession prompted by a missionary's sermon and his kids' music constitutes a bona fide conversion that will result in our seeing them in heaven. All I know is they came, great waves of Japanese men and women and children streaming toward the trailer where workers led them in the sinner's prayer, gave them a Gospel of John and the address of a church. This happened wherever we set up the trailer and passed out the tracts, and it was enough to convince a four-year-old missionary that despite the separation from all that seemed so comfortable and familiar, this was where we had to be; this was what we had to do.

That's not to say I never got homesick. In fact, much of the time I was lonely, and the separation from the folks back home never seemed as wide as when we received a tape of Gramma's voice giving us news from the home front. When it arrived in the mail, Daddy would get out the old Wollensack tape recorder and set it on the coffee table in our small living room. Each of us would crowd around him as he placed the reel onto the left spindle of the machine and threaded the tape around pulleys and through a special slot that led to still another pulley and then the "take up reel." Then he would push the "play" button and after a few seconds of hissing, Gramma's voice would greet us, and a big lump would form in my throat. I would close my eyes and try to imagine her sitting next to me on the couch in our Winona Lake parsonage with her hankie tucked into the sleeve of her blouse. I imagined myself climbing up onto her lap and snuggling close as she kept right on talking to my daddy.

After a few minutes of Gramma talking on the tape, we would suddenly hear a congregation singing. Gramma had taken her tape recorder to church to record the Sunday service, then cornered people on the way out to say hello to her son, Dale, who was a missionary in Japan. We always laughed when a voice asked, "How are ya doing, Dale," and then paused for several seconds, expecting a response. He forgot that his voice was on a tape that would be mailed via "boat mail," arriving two to three months later. But that never really mattered to us.

We also got tapes from Mamma's folks. How Grandma and Grandpa Gates found a tape recorder in Mesick, Michigan, is beyond me. They heated with and cooked on wood stoves and had a phone that you cranked a couple of times to get the operator's attention so she could hook you up with, say, Aunt Gwen up near Briar Hill, about three miles away. But somehow they got hold of a tape recorder and made a tape. Grandma did most of the talking, but Grandpa sang "I Did It," a comical old tune that was his trademark, and then told us he would make buttermilk pancakes and backfat for us when we got back.

We would play those tapes over and over again, and even though they were supposed to help us not feel so lonesome, they had just the opposite effect on me. I never felt so far way as when I listened to my grandparents' voices on the tape recorder.

The other thing that made me lonesome was going to church. Most Sundays we were on the road, conducting crusades. But occasionally, we would have a free Sunday and go to church at Chapel Center, a large church for ecumenical services at the army base in

Tokyo. I loved these Sundays because they represented the closest thing to what Sunday had been for me back in Winona Lake. A real organ and the singing of hymns and Americans all dressed up to worship God. Even though it wasn't quite the same, walking into that church on the army base made me miss the white pews and red carpet of the only other church I had ever known; the one I lived in.

After the service was over, we usually took a carload of GIs home with us for a nice home-cooked Sunday dinner. It seemed like the Sundays we were home, our house was always full of young soldiers. One Sunday, as Mamma cleared the table, I slid out of my chair, walked over to one of the visiting servicemen, and climbed up onto his lap.

"Why are you brown?" I asked, as Daddy kind of coughed real loud.

The soldier's answer made me feel inferior for years.

"Well you know, before God sends us down here, he has to bake us. When he put most folks in his oven up there in heaven, he took them out too soon and they looked all pale and white. But the rest of us he left in for just the right amount of time, and we came out looking s-o-o-o-o beautiful."

We stayed in Japan for nearly three years, preaching the gospel in open air rallies, in prisons and reformatories, and in the handful of small churches that had been established by a previous generation of missionaries. Every weekend that we weren't home was an adventure, which is probably why I was a little disappointed when my daddy told us it was time to go back to America. On the one hand, I couldn't wait to see my grandparents, but it would mean saying good-bye to my best friends. Memories of Winona Lake were fading, and from what I heard of my parents' conversations, we weren't going back there anyway.

We left the work of our Lord in the capable hands of people like Ted Engstrom and Sam Wolgemuth and Norm Overland and Sister Milliken and, of course, nationals like Bishop Oda and Jingo-san and Isamu and others. It was hard to bid them farewell because they had become like family to me. But it was harder to say good-bye to Hako-chan, my best friend for three years. We lived across the alley from each other and spent the endless hours that only youth affords catching cicadas, exploring the bamboo forest behind our home, riding our bikes, and sneaking into the underground bomb shelter in a neighbor's home across the street.

For the most part, we played in silence broken occasionally by laughter since neither of us spoke the other's language. By the time we left Japan, however, both of us had learned a new language well enough to communicate in either English or Japanese. It worked like this. Once or twice a week, Hako-chan would come up to my bedroom where we would page through *Life* magazine together. Every missionary box included a few back issues of *Life* or *The Saturday Evening Post*. When we came to a picture of something familiar to both of us—say, a cat—he would point to it and say, "Nekko," and I would respond by saying, "Cat." Then we would turn the pages until we came to another recognizable object, and repeat the words to each other. That is how we taught each other our languages.

One day, we were paging through a Bible storybook and we came to the familiar (to me, anyway) picture of Jesus hanging on the cross between two thieves. I pointed to Him and said, "Jesus." When he responded by saying "Jesus," I realized he had no name in his language for Jesus and that this was probably the first time he had ever said that name. All the theology and doctrine I had gotten from six years of churchgoing told me that this was a sacred moment, an opportunity not to be ignored. This one moment may have been the only reason I came to Japan.

I pointed to my heart and said the name of our Savior again, and he did the same. He pointed to his heart and then looked me right in the eye and smiled broadly as he said "Jesus."

I have been back to Japan twice, but only to change planes at Narita airport. If I could go back to Tokyo, I would like to find Hako-chan and ask him if he remembers.

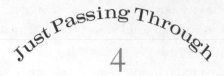

Just Passing Through

4

"And I can't feel at home in this world anymore."

◦∽

M*y daddy was either very wise or just plain crazy when he decided how* we would get home to America from Japan. I have gotten to know him better over the past forty years and have concluded that he was both.

We came to Japan on the *U.S.S. President Wilson,* a passenger liner that left from San Francisco with six of us crammed into two small cabins and our Ford Ranch Wagon in the cargo hold. It must have been a good way to travel because Daddy announced that we would return the same way. Actually, it ended up being three ships—*Asia, Taegleberg,* and *Nieu Amsterdam*—heading home the long way around the world through the Pacific Ocean, East China Sea, South China Sea, dipping down into the Indian Ocean, Arabian Sea, through the Gulf of Aden, and up into the Mediterranean Sea via the Suez Canal at a time when military escorts were necessary. At Genoa, we caught a train that took us up through Italy, Switzerland, Germany, and Holland where we crossed the Channel and for the first time in three years were surrounded by people who spoke our language, only to board another ship for the journey home.

When we finally arrived in New York City, I cracked up the passengers on our city bus ride to Grand Central Station when I asked my daddy in a rather loud voice, "Now that we're in America, can we eat apples with the skins on them?"

I had not meant to be funny. Despite the precautions of adding Halizone tablets to purify our drinking water, peeling all fruit and vegetables, and regularly washing the skin right off our hands, I contracted an especially virulent form of amoebic dysentery that required an antibiotic that was unavailable in Japan. I have since learned that I was close to death for a few days, forcing my parents to their knees in between frantic calls to military bases and the U.S. Embassy until the medicine arrived by special courier.

Bill, my oldest brother, suffered a ruptured appendix and also hovered between life and death in a primitive hospital staffed by physicians who could not speak English. Our first night in Japan was interrupted with loud shouting and threats from a drunken patriot who was still fighting the war his country had lost to our side, and on another afternoon, Dale slipped and broke his arm as he was trying to get away from a gun-wielding neighbor boy. My parents were not especially brave or heroic but accepted these and other close calls as the special turf of those who answered the call to foreign missions. We were, after all, descendants of the apostle who had been shipwrecked and imprisoned while carrying the gospel abroad. I wouldn't go so far as to say we welcomed disaster in order to earn our stripes as missionaries, but when it approached we did not run from it.

One Saturday we packed the car for a day-long journey to the village of Taira where Daddy would preach the next day. Halfway there, we discovered that our gas tank had developed a small leak. Not only was it dangerous—"One spark and we could all be killed," Daddy warned after crawling out from beneath the car—but there were not enough gas stations along the way to keep a leaky tank supplied.

We must have been quite a sight in that small Japanese village— six light-skinned people stranded alongside the road in an American car. Daddy was pacing back and forth, and Mamma had that look in her eyes that said, "I'm really scared to death but for the kids' sake I'm not going to show it." If Mesick, Michigan, seemed a long ways away to her, Winona Lake felt like the other side of the universe to me. All I could think about was that car blowing up with me in it.

When we learned that there were no mechanics in the little village where we had stopped and it was clear that the leak could not be repaired just then, Daddy got back in the car, meaning we should get back in too. Then with a look I had seen so often before—a look that included the faces of all who had to hear the gospel tomorrow—Daddy started the engine, slipped the dusty station wagon into gear, and began singing:

"My Lord knows the way through the wilderness . . ."

Five other voices joined in:

> And all I have to do is follow.
> My Lord knows the way through the wilderness,
> And all I have to do is follow.
> Strength for today, is mine alway',
> And all that I need for tomorrow.
> My Lord knows the way through the wilderness.
> And all I have to do is follow.

Without missing a beat, he started another:

> One day as I was walking
> Down a lonesome road,
> An angel came unto me

45

And this is what he told.

I loved this one, especially the part where Daddy would sing,
"King Jesus got His arms all around me,
No evil thought can harm me,
For I thank God I'm in His care."

By now we were in another village and, wouldn't you know it,
we found a gas station with a mechanic on duty who went to work
on the gas tank and plugged the leak and had us on our way, only
two hours behind schedule. You could not have told me then (or
now) that an angel did not reach down and keep the leak from
draining the tank or worse, exploding and killing us all, and that
another angel did not settle down ahead of us to make sure a gas
station was on our way and that it was open and that a mechanic
would be there just waiting to fix the gas tank on an American car.
And the reason all of these things just happened was because God
wanted some of his children in Taira to hear the gospel for the first
time in their lives, and we were the only ones available in that part
of the world on that weekend to do it and there might never be
another chance. Ever. That is what we believed every day of the
nearly three years that we were missionaries in Japan.

In fact, one of the most important spiritual lessons I learned
from my missionary-kid days was that when you do what God asks
you to do, he takes care of you. I did not know it then, but I have
since learned that we were not just missionaries but poor missionaries, something of a redundancy. Our sponsoring agency, Youth
for Christ, sent Daddy a small check. Other than that, we were on
our own. We barely had enough money to buy food and clothing,
which is why there was so much excitement when a "missionary
box" arrived. My daddy would drive down to the shipping dock
and pick up the cardboard barrel that had arrived from our home

church and when he got back to our home my older brothers would help him carry it into the living room. Despite our eagerness to tear into its contents, we would always have to wait until Daddy thanked Jesus for his goodness to us. Then he would pry the top off the barrel and start pulling the contents out and laying them on the *tatami* grass mat floor: reversible winter jackets for my little brother and me; brand new (never worn by another kid) blue jeans that I could "grow into"; an umbrella that I slept with the first night after it arrived; flannel bathrobes from Mearl and Frank Bradley (that I still have and that every one of my own kids have worn); a yellow plastic toy car with doors, a hood, and trunk that opened; a stuffed Easter bunny that I carried the rest of the way around the world; Kelloggs Frosted Flakes.

Bill was a teenager, so you can imagine his reaction one Christmas to pulling out a box with his name on it and finding inside a pair of blue suede shoes. Even though we were four thousand miles away from Memphis, he had heard all about Elvis. That same year, Dale got a little bug collecting kit, and Rik got a pretend doctor's kit, which he used on our cat. Daddy made sure we knew that all this stuff came from people back in America who were helping us preach the gospel to the Japanese.

It seemed as if almost monthly there was some kind of mishap that could have ended much worse than it actually did. Whenever we were confronted with bad news, the first things my parents did was pray, and though this may sound like so much evangelical hyperbole, I do not ever recall a single unanswered prayer.

But now it was time to leave, and we were in Yokohama, standing alongside the railing on the top deck of the *Asia,* a ship flying under the Turkish flag that would take us on our first leg home. We threw colored paper streamers to our friends on the dock who had gathered to bid us farewell, and it was probably one of the saddest moments in my young life. To this day I have a hard time saying good-bye, even to friends I know I will see again soon, and I think it goes back to seeing those ribbons break as the ship pulled away from the dock and watching my Japanese "family" weeping and waving, knowing we would never see each other again, which we haven't.

Soon enough, we were on the open sea on an adventure that would change my life forever. The ships my daddy put us on were freighters with passenger accommodations, which meant we stopped at nearly every port along the way. We anchored in Hong Kong harbor where I saw a giant shark leap out of the water and almost take the arm off a dock hand. We took launches into port cities like Bombay and Karachi and Aden and Jiddah and Port Said.

In the Suez Canal I tossed a piece of string over the railing and an Italian kitchen worker on the deck below tied a dinner roll on the end of the string. When he tugged it, I was sure I had a fish. Occasionally I would sneak into the hold with one of my brothers as we tried to make conversation with the African cargo handlers. In ports along the way, we saw holy men and prostitutes. Beggars with children they had intentionally crippled to attract more hand-outs. Women sitting in gutters chewing betel nut as they held out little tin cups. Brown-skinned children swimming in the water next to our anchored ship. They would call out to us to throw coins into the water, then they would dive to retrieve them before the silvery discs hit bottom.

One time, a British tourist traveling on our ship threw a washer instead of a coin into the water, and I learned a lesson in physics and depravity. Because of its hole the washer shot down much faster to the bottom, causing the boys to dive deeper repeatedly as they tried to find the "coin," which bent the tourist over in laughter. I thought it was the cruelest thing I had seen in my young life because my daddy had explained that this was how these children got enough money to buy food for their families.

We walked shoeless in Indian temples, traced chariot tracks on Pompeii, and took Communion in Westminster Abbey. We visited a storefront church in Hong Kong where the only light was a motorcycle headlight clipped to a wire that ran down to a car battery behind the makeshift pulpit. If we ever encountered someone who looked like they needed the gospel—and to Daddy that usually meant someone who looked poor or sick—we gave them some money and a tract and tried to tell them about Jesus.

You do not see these things without knowing for certain that you are a small part of something huge and wonderful that began before time.

By the time I was seven years old, I had lived in four homes in two different countries, sailed through a typhoon and a monsoon, carried my daddy's camera bag on four continents, and eventually was awakened early on a foggy morning as our ship steamed into New York Harbor.

"We're home," Daddy said as he pointed to the bronze lady who had welcomed so many immigrants. It was neat to see the "Statue of Liberty," but for some reason it did not feel like home yet.

We caught a train in Grand Central Station and rolled along for twenty-six hours down the coast until just outside of Saint Petersburg, Florida, where the clickety-clack of the iron wheels against the tracks grew slower and slower, which made me almost shake with excitement. The last time I had seen Gramma I was three years old, but when I saw the white-haired lady standing on the platform in a creme-colored suit with a matching pillbox hat, I knew it was her. Her home on fourteenth Street became ours for a few weeks until we moved into another parsonage closer to the First Free Methodist Church of Saint Petersburg, Florida, and I became a PK all over again. Then my daddy was called to a more important church job in Michigan, in a small town called Spring Arbor, and we moved again. Shortly after we got settled into yet another home, we got one of those calls late at night that sets kids straining to listen but not really wanting to hear because if Mamma and Daddy are crying, the news must be pretty bad.

My gramma's body arrived by train, and when we went to see her at the Horne-Vinson funeral home she was wearing that same creme-colored suit she wore on the train platform. The next day, a large black hearse brought my grandmother to the old stone church in our new hometown where a group of men carried it to the front. After the service, they carried her back out, put her in the hearse, and drove one block to the cemetery where she was put in the ground.

That is when I cried. My daddy must have realized how upsetting it was for a young boy to see something like that, and even though he was crying too, he leaned down to tell me that Gramma wasn't really inside that hole. Then he told me that his mother was home now, and that was when I first realized why even though I was back in America I did not feel at home. And that is why I can sit in my own home today and watch my kids grow up before my eyes and feel both a peaceful contentment and a strange longing at the same time.

Very few members of my generation live in the same towns where they were born. We went off to college and if we were lucky, bought an old Volkswagon minibus, painted flowers on the side of it, and drove off in search of meaning. Eventually we gave in to economics and made success our new destination. It has been a journey that has included new addresses, new neighborhoods, new schools, new friends, and new churches. Unlike our parents (excluding preachers), we did not stay with the same job until we got the watch, but were either downsized or retooled as a chang-ing world demanded skills beyond our liberal arts degrees. For me, it has meant twelve homes and six jobs in three states in twenty-eight years of marriage, and a fair amount of guilt, especially when our oldest son confided in his twenty-first year that he felt as if he really didn't have a home.

He does, of course, just as we all do.

We're just not there yet.

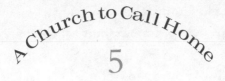

A Church to Call Home

5

"Wonderful riches more than tongue can tell."

❧

S*ince my daddy was now a church administrator, he traveled to other* churches each Sunday. Sometimes we all went with him, but most Sundays, Mamma stayed home so that her boys could finally have a "church home." The nicest thing about that was technically I wasn't the preacher's kid. In other words, I could just be an ordinary kid. Sort of. The first Sunday in my new church I had to dress up in the kimonos with my brothers and sing "Jesus Loves Me" in Japanese in front of the whole church. After an introduction like that, you're never ordinary.

"Why'd you wear a dress to church?" asked a boy my age after the service. He and about five other guys were waiting for me under a huge mulberry tree next to the driveway that separated the church from the parsonage. They would eventually become good friends, but first there was a little business to take care of.

"It's not a dress, it's a kimono," I answered. "In Japan, that's what everybody wears."

"Yeah, well it still looks like a dress to me," he countered, which got his buddies laughing. I didn't really blame them. It wasn't my idea to do this, but on the other hand I didn't like being laughed at.

"You bein' a Jap and all, I'll bet you know judo." He said it with a smile, but I could feel myself getting angry.

"I'm not Japanese, and they're not called Japs, but I do know judo. Wanna see?"

I didn't really know judo, though we had gone to Sumo wrestling matches in Japan, and I was pretty quick on my feet. Before he could answer I somehow slid my right leg in front of his left foot, grabbed his arm, turned, and flipped him over my shoulder and onto his back with a thud. He quickly got back up, eyes watering a little but otherwise no worse for the wear. His buddies closed in on both of us, wondering what would happen next.

"Wow, that was neat!" he said. That was my introduction to the Teft Road gang that included Jimmy Stewart and his brother Tommy, Elden Bennett, Mike Barrows, and Doug Johnson.

We lived about a block from the church, an old stone building with a steeple and a huge iron bell that called the village of Spring Arbor to worship every Sunday morning and night, and back again on Wednesday night. I may have been spoiled by all the rallies in Japan because even though I liked the idea of finally having my own church, it seemed pretty boring. And slow.

Everything about church seemed to be just outside the reach of whatever age I was at the time. For example, I loved singing the opening hymn, which was almost always "A Mighty Fortress." The old Hammond organ would roll through the introduction, its amplifier powering two huge speakers hanging on either side of the platform, as the song leader simply lifted his hands to pull us to our feet. But two verses would have been more to my liking than four. And for some reason, the tempo slowed with each verse so that by the time we got to "His kingdom is forever . . . ," we sort of knew what forever meant.

After the opening hymn came something called the responsive reading. These were readings printed in the back of the hymnal with alternate sentences printed in bold type. The preacher would read the bold, followed by the congregation reading the regular type. The readings were straight from the Bible, and because it was the King James Version it just seemed like a lot of thees and thous and verilys. What made it worse is that we had been standing since the first thunderous chord of the opening hymn. It was about halfway through the responsive reading that I would often lean over for relief with my elbows on the pew in front of me, only to be gently pulled back up to attention by my mamma's hand on my collar.

You could almost hear a collective sigh of relief from the congregation when the song leader told us we could be seated as the organist started playing the next hymn. It was usually a slower, more somber selection so as to quiet our souls for the pastoral prayer. By now, every kid in the sanctuary had selected a daydreaming topic that would be put to good use for the next five minutes.

My first pastor other than my daddy was a man named Verdon Dunckel, whom everyone called Uncle Dunk. In so many ways he was the perfect pastor for young and old—gregarious, youthful, and fun, but so wise and committed to serving God. When it came to the pastoral prayer, however, Uncle Dunk tested our already waning patience. For him, and many pastors of his generation, the pastoral prayer was an art form, second only in importance to the sermon. It was almost like the warm-up to the sermon, and it was as comprehensive as it was long.

Uncle Dunk always started in our little village, lifting up our local needs before taking us all over the world, naming every missionary and government leader he knew, which were many. He'd pray by name for anyone feeling even slightly under the weather, and he'd pray for the families of those who'd lost a loved one during the week. If for some reason you had missed out on the local gossip, you got caught up on most of it during the pastoral prayer. He'd publicly thank the Lord for "the many blessings you have bestowed upon us your children" and then list them. He'd remind the Lord (and the rest of us) that we were once horrible sinners, and my ears would perk up as he would mention the kinds of sins from which we'd been saved.

His prayers had a rhythm that was almost musical and often seemed dependent upon the response from the congregation. So, for example, if he got a few "amens" when he asked God to protect us from evil, he'd hammer that theme hard:

"You *know* the condition of this sin-sick world, oh Lord."

Two or three amens.

"The wickedness in Hollywood that beckons to our precious young people."

More amens, with a few "yes Lords" and maybe a "have mercy."

"The liquor industry as it reaches its tentacles even into our little village through a proposal that will go before the county commissioners allowing stores to sell this poison here!"

All of the above, in greater volume, plus a couple "help us, Jesuses."

It didn't take you many Sundays to begin recognizing certain parishioners by their unique contributions during prayer. One dear sister would moan "Ooooooh, precious Jesus" several times, while a guy everyone called Pop would rear back and cut loose with "hallelujah" after about every third sentence or so. My fourth-grade Sunday school teacher would just sort of groan in a low, guttural voice, but if you listened closely you heard phrases like "wash us in your blood" and "bless your name."

You even got variations on the amens. One camp would put the accent on the second syllable, giving it a sort of triumphant resonance: "aMEN!" The other camp always sounded to me a little more spiritual because they would accent the first syllable and let the "men" sort of trail off, dropping a few notes in volume and pitch. In both cases, the "A" was a long vowel, rhyming with hay. If this was one of the more liberal or liturgical churches, it would have been pronounced ah-men, and only the pastor ever said it.

The pastoral prayer always wound down to an artful segue into the Lord's prayer, though if you were a visitor you had to be alert: "And we ask these thing in the precious name of your son who taught us to pray . . ."

We always used "debts" instead of "trespasses," at the part that says, "Lord forgive us . . . ," which created bonus amusement for us kids if a visitor happened to be present from a church that used "trespasses." Nothing like hearing someone bellow out in the brief pause after "debts": "our tresspa . . . um, debts."

You might get the impression from the lively response of the congregation during the pastoral prayer that we were charismatic. We were not. If we had been, the pastor would have ended each sentence with an extra syllable rhyming with "uh." In other words, "You know the sin-sick condition of the world, oh Lord," would become "You know the sin-sick condition of the world, oh Lord-uh." I don't know why they did that, but they did.

My particular denomination was one that grew out of "the holiness movement," which in those days shared a lot with Pentecostals but took an abrupt left turn when it came to speaking in tongues (absolutely prohibited) and on-the-spot instantaneous healing (we always gave the Lord some wiggle room by praying "if it be your will" before asking him to heal us). And generally, our services were much tamer than the "holy rollers," as we smugly called them. In fact, a good way for a pastor to loose his ministerial credentials in our denomination was for him to "go charismatic." So while some of the saints would get worked up now and then, it was all kept pretty much under control, except when the spirit decided to move upon a dear saint, Olive Woolsey.

You could not anticipate or prepare for the moment when the spirit of our Lord descended upon Sister Woolsey. It could happen anytime—during the pastoral prayer, after the male quartet sang, or even right in the middle of announcements. You might be mulling over a daydream topic or coloring in the closed spaces in the letters on the bulletin or covertly writing a note to shove under the pew ahead of you to one of your friends when it happened.

"Oooooooooooo-hooo-hooo-hooooooooooooo!"

It was Olive, and it always scared me, no matter how many times I'd heard it. The pastor would step away from the pulpit and sort of bow his head, and everyone else would follow suit except for us kids who craned our necks to make sure it was only Olive and not the real thing. We had all heard that when the Lord returns, the angel Gabriel will blow long and hard on his horn. We also knew that when that happened, "two shall be taken while the other left behind," and I think we just wanted to make sure no one was missing from our midst while we were still there. Olive might clap her white-gloved hands over her head and let out another wail that sounded a lot like one of the professional mourners I saw at a funeral pyre in Bombay in our missionary days, and then she'd settle down with "Oh bless me Jesus," and there would be this corporate shifting in our seats and clearing of throats and the pastor would step back up to the pulpit and take up where he left off:

"There will be a potluck Friday night at the fire barn sponsored by the Junior Missionary Society."

I once asked my dad why she did that and he said it was because she was so overjoyed and overcome at the thought of Jesus dying on the cross for her sins. He called it "getting blessed." It sort of made sense to me, but I wondered what people thought who were visiting our church for the first time. If it scared a regular like me, I could only guess what it did to them. I can't say that it bothered me a whole lot, but for the first time I realized that some of what we did in church was kind of embarrassing.

By the time Uncle Dunk stepped to the pulpit to preach, most of us kids were finished. Whatever went on over the next hour went on without us. We were present in body only, as we devised ways to entertain ourselves without disrupting the service or looking as if we weren't paying attention. Games like hangman and tic-tac-toe were tough because they usually entailed passing a sheet of paper—usually the offering envelopes that were stuffed into little holders on the back of the pew—back and forth, which was off limits. If you leaned over with your elbows on your knees in a prayerful posture, you might get away with unscrewing one of the screws that held the hymnbook rack in place, but if you got carried away and the rack fell off the pew, you were in big trouble.

Mamma did her best to give us activities that, in her mind, seemed more spiritual or at least less disruptive. One of her favorites was to take out her hankie and fold and roll it in such a way that it became two babies in a hammock. That was good for about two minutes. She also would write a Bible verse on the top of a piece of paper and tell us to see how many words we could make out of it. Or she would make a scribble on a piece of paper and tell us to turn it into a picture that illustrated the topic of the sermon. Mine always ended up looking like a bigger scribble.

Everyone carried a Bible to church, and if you slipped your Sunday school "take-home paper" inside of it just right, you might get away with reading it, since you could always read your Bible during a sermon. Nothing pleased the adults more than seeing a kid hunkered over an open Bible during the sermon. As the years went by, Mamma mellowed a bit and let us actually read our take-home papers in church. All, that is, except for a handout we received about once a month called *Sunday Pix*. Our regular Sunday school take-home paper, *Story Trails,* was about an eight-page collection of stories designed to capture your imagination while teaching you something about the Bible. It seemed a little heavier on the Bible than imagination, though you could always count on at least one good story.

Sunday Pix, on the other hand, was a full-color magazine that dangerously resembled a comic book and was loaded with really exciting stories. Because it was so colorful and could be mistaken for a comic book, we never dared read it in church. For some reason I'll never understand, comic books were forbidden in our house, except for a series called "Classic Illustrated," which were the classics of literature put to cartoonlike drawings. The funny thing about this is that whenever we visited Uncle Loren and Aunt Francis, the couple who were instrumental in my daddy's return to faith, we rushed up to their kids' attic bedroom in search of the forbidden: a box that contained not only dozens of the latest comic books but *Mad* magazine to boot! But when it came to reading material for church, *Sunday Pix* was out.

One year, word filtered down from the high schoolers that you could play a really neat game with the hymnbook. The idea was to page through the hymnal and see what happened if you added the words "between the sheets" after the title of a hymn. It seemed too wicked to do that with any hymn whose title bore the name of Jesus, but when you got to hymns like "Glorious Things of Thee Are Spoken" or "Love Divine," it was hard to keep from laughing out loud, which of course always got us a stern look from Mamma.

When Uncle Dunk finally said, "In conclusion . . . ," we knew we only had about ten more minutes left, but those became the longest ten minutes of the entire morning. By now, even our parents had given up trying to make us listen, letting us color in all the closed spaces on the typing in the bulletin or maybe even folding it into a paper airplane. It gave little comfort to look around and see some of the men either jerking their heads upright in response to their wives' elbow to the ribs or in a chin-to-the-chest position of surrender. On Sunday morning at 11:45, the hardest parts about being a Christian were hunger, boredom, and fatigue.

After Uncle Dunk finished preaching, the song leader would announce the final hymn and the collective sigh signified unanimous approval. Naturally, we had to sing all five verses, only to be followed by the benediction, which for Uncle Dunk and many ministers like him, was a last chance to get his point across. The main difference between the pastor praying and preaching is that most people had their eyes open when he preached.

Finally, we all sang one more time, which might explain why the *Doxology* is close to my favorite song of all times because it meant within a half hour we would be sitting down to pot roast.

The victory, however, was short-lived. After dinner, there was not much we were allowed to do except take a nap, work on a jigsaw puzzle, or play a table game. And then, after toasted-cheese sandwiches, it was back to church for another round of singing, praying, and listening to a sermon. Only Sunday nights added two features that made life a little more interesting.

First, there was lots of singing, which I always liked, but even more so on Sunday nights because in addition to hymns, we sang gospel choruses. Songs like "Love Lifted Me," "Showers of Blessing," and "In My Heart There Rings a Melody." The one song that got everyone going was "Wonderful Grace of Jesus," which had a fast-moving line that the men got to sing all by themselves on the chorus. During the week, Harold Trevan would paint houses, and

Bill Gilbertson would fix your car, and Russ Brugger would sell you insurance, and Brad Phipps would make camshafts, and Elwin Johnson would drive the fire truck, and Bruce Davenport would give you a shot of penicillin, and Jim Mannoia would teach religion at the college across the street, but on Sunday nights they became a chorus of men singing,

> Higher than a mountain,
> Sparkling like a fountain,
> All sufficient grace for even me.

On a real good Sunday night, the song leader invited anyone from the congregation to call out the page number of their favorite song, and that's when some of us decided to add a little fun to the service. We would start paging through the hymnal, looking for the most obscure, unfamiliar hymn we could find. As others shouted out the old favorites like "Jesus Saves" and "The Old Rugged Cross," one of us kids would call out a page number, then watch the song leader's face when he turned to "Commit Thou All Thy Grief" or "That Day of Wrath, That Dreadful Day."

The other feature that made Sunday nights worth missing *The Wonderful World of Disney* was the testimony service. This was when the song leader announced a song and then said, "Now after this number we're going to give you a chance to tell us what the Lord's done for you lately."

The song would end, and then there would be this period of awkward silence. Then either Orville Fitzgerald, the town barber, or Pop Young, a local contractor, would break the ice. If we were lucky, someone with a real bad "sin story" would take over next. This would usually be someone who had just gotten saved recently and held us captive mostly with the descriptions of how sinful they had actually been. I loved those stories, not just because we got to hear about a lot of drinking and smoking, and maybe some sex or gambling, but because they made you feel not so bad about your own little sins. It made you feel that if someone that bad off could be a Christian, you must be one too.

Still, if it had been up to me, I would have been home on Sunday evenings watching either *Bonanza, Wonderful World of Disney,* or *The Ed Sullivan Show.* Believe it or not, once, when I was about twelve, I got my wish, and with Mamma's blessing.

Daddy was out of town, as usual, and wouldn't be home until around midnight. The Beatles had just invaded America and were to perform on *The Ed Sullivan Show.* Mamma was not into Beatlemania, but my little brother, Rik, and I were. We started our campaign early in the week, first begging, then promising all sorts of work around the house. We were certain it was a hopeless cause, but we kept at it just the same. We had used the same arguments and tactics for *Disney* and *Bonanza*:

"All my friends get to watch them." (Bad argument—if everybody was doing it, that was reason enough not to do it.)

"Just this once." (She knew you couldn't close Pandora's box.)

"Church is boring." (Guaranteed not to work.)

"This only happens once in a lifetime."

Maybe that's why she relented. Or maybe she was just worn down without Daddy around to back her up. In any event, Dorothy Cryderman let her two youngest sons, Lyn and Rik, skip Sunday night church to watch the Beatles on *The Ed Sullivan Show.*

True to her word, however, that's the only time I can remember being allowed to miss church on Sunday night. For the first 1,000 Sundays of my life, I don't think I missed more than ten Sundays of church attendance—morning and evening—which is not a bad record.

We went to church because our parents made us go, and they went to church because it was what you did on Sunday. Small-town America took a sabbatical once a week; it shut down for worship and rest. In most towns and even small cities, it was hard to find a business that stayed open on Sundays. Since my Dad drove across the state to visit other churches on Sunday, he always made sure his gas tank was full on Saturday night because he might not find a gas station open the next day. Even if you weren't a Christian, you were forced to slow down on Sunday if only because just about everybody else did.

But I didn't want to slow down, which is probably why I liked Sunday school so much.

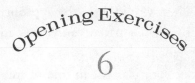

6

"Climb, climb up sunshine mountain."

ೲ

O*ne of the reasons church seemed so boring was because we entered the* hallowed sanctuary straight from Sunday school. Where church was a place you had to whisper, in Sunday school you could shout and nobody got worried that you might be going charismatic. In fact, you usually got rewarded for it.

Sunday school began with something called "opening exercises," led by a person known as the "Sunday school superintendent." It almost always took place "upstairs," which meant the sanctuary. To a kid, church was divided into upstairs and downstairs. Upstairs was mostly for adults, while downstairs was for kids, the exception being opening exercises.

The routine was pretty simple. You'd play in the parking lot or on the church lawn while the adults gathered around the church door and talked. When Guy Priest (that really was his name) started pulling on the thick rope that rang the church bell, you'd head inside to the sanctuary and find your section, which was a row or two of pews reserved for your class. Classes were organized around age groups or grades, and they were always segregated by gender.

So the fourth-grade boys would have their row, the sixth-grade girls, and so on. Teachers would sit in the appropriate rows and do their best to keep order, while parents and other adults would sit in the back half of the sanctuary.

If you were lucky, your class sat in one of the front rows with the little earphones hanging on the back of the pew in front of you. These were for older people who were hard of hearing, but during opening exercises we would surreptitiously turn up the volume control to try and get a little feedback whistling out of them, a fairly dumb church crime because you were so easily caught by the teacher.

The purpose of opening exercises seemed to be twofold: take care of business and warm us up for the classroom time that followed. Business always included recognizing those who had celebrated birthdays during the previous week. Whether you were eight or eighty, you were called to the front, given a pencil, followed by the entire church singing "Happy Birthday."

If you brought a friend to Sunday school, you also got a pencil, as did your guest. If you knew your memory verse, guess what you got? If you were real lucky, you brought a friend on your birthday and said your memory verse: three pencils. Naturally, the pencils were never sharpened, for that might tempt you to write in church. If you visited my home in Spring Arbor and opened the drawer next to the phone where we stuffed anything that had no other place, you would find at least a dozen church pencils at any given time.

If you have not guessed already, Sunday school attendance was a big deal, and we did two things to promote it. For the regulars, there were the Sunday school attendance awards in the form of interlocking pins that would hang vertically from your lapel. These pins were the sole incentive for perfect attendance in a given year, usually awarded on "rally day," which was sort of the kick off for a new season in the fall and not to be confused with "promotion day," a Sunday in June where you were promoted up to the next grade. Your first pin bore the words, "Sunday School," with a smaller metal bar hanging below it that said, "Perfect Attendance." Then, for each successive year of not missing a single Sunday, you would receive another little "Perfect Attendance" bar to hang below the previous one. It was not unusual on "rally day" to see at least one older gentleman with a chain of perfect attendance pins dangling below his waist standing next to the rest of us kids who might have only two or three year's worth of pins hanging from our lapels. I'm not making any of this up.

The other way we promoted Sunday school attendance was the Sunday school contest. While there were many variations on this venerable institution, the most common was simply the challenge to break the attendance record. Let's say your church normally averaged around 150 in Sunday school with an all-time high attendance of 227, which you could bet happened on Easter. The pastor and Sunday school superintendent would put their heads together and come up with an outlandish goal: 300 people in Sunday school by the end of the month.

During opening exercises for the next four Sundays we would all wait to see how high the "temperature" would rise on the attendance thermometer that stood from floor to ceiling off to the side of the platform, temporarily covering up that wooden board that listed the hymns we would sing later in the worship service, the pastor's sermon topic, and for some strange reason, the amount of money collected in last Sunday's offering.

Anticipation would build, beginning with the first Sunday when the red indicator climbed to 219. The next Sunday you guessed by all the kids getting pencils that this would be a record, and you were right: 231! By the time another Sunday rolled around, you figured you'd be within a handful of the all-time record for Sunday school attendance, and you were already mentally noting who you could bring to help break the record on the fourth and final Sunday. Imagine the letdown when the thermometer actually slid down a few notches: 228. Time to pull out the big guns, or more accurately, the big gun. The challenge. The all-or-nothing laying down of the gauntlet by the pastor to the congregation. These were the pivotal points in every Sunday school contest that produced the kind of newspaper headlines that Jay Leno would die for, had he been on late-night television back then: "Preacher to Kiss a Pig if Record Falls" or "Pastor to Wear Dress if Church Hits 300" or "Come Throw a Pie at Pastor Wilson Next Sunday." Somehow, it worked, because I cannot remember a single contest where we did not nudge the thermometer up over the top.

It's a wonder we actually grew during contests because in our small town, nearly everyone attended Sunday school. Still, all of us had a pagan friend or two who came in handy in times like these, though at a price. They may have been without the Lord, but they were not without brains. I lost half my baseball card collection to Ernie Wilkinson one year in a bidding war with my church buddies, just to get him to come and be counted.

Another friend, who I only remember as Dennis, was a member of the town's only Seventh-day Adventist family. On the one hand we envied him because he could play ball on Sunday and also because some really good television programs were on Sunday night. On the other hand, there was something almost sacred about Saturdays that none of us would want to ruin by having to go to church. Good old Dennis always seemed available to help out during a contest, but the catch was he insisted that whoever invited him to our church had to go the following Saturday to *his* church. It was a fair request, and I wish I had taken him up on it, but never

68

did, partly because I just couldn't bring myself to miss playing on Saturday, but also because we were taught that Seventh-day Adventism was a false religion. I never knew what made them so dangerous to people from my tradition, but I suspected it had something to do with the fact that they were vegetarians. I don't recall Dennis ever helping us win an attendance contest.

I *do* recall David Peebles helping out once, which was a minor miracle. David Peebles was about the toughest guy in town. I can hardly remember a Saturday on which he didn't beat me up. He also smoked and swore and made fun of the rest of us for going to church while he went fishing at Lime Lake or watched cartoons. True, we could watch cartoons on Saturday, but Sunday's cartoons were always better, if only because they were forbidden.

David was so bad that even when a Sunday school contest rolled around, we were too afraid to invite him. But one year I must have been desperate. The details are clouded by time, but what most likely happened was that after the first three Sundays of the contest I was zero for three, which probably meant I had forgotten to invite anyone. It also meant that the pool of pagans was pretty shallow. I was usually good for at least one or two visitors, so my church friends were counting on me to come through. That left me with little choice but to invite David Peebles. In addition to being the town bully, David was our paperboy, so when he came to collect one Saturday morning, I intercepted him on the front porch and asked him: "Hey David, why don't you come to Sunday school with me tomorrow?" I was slightly encouraged by the fact that he didn't get off his bike and put me in a headlock.

"You know I don't go to church," he sneered.

"Oh, you won't have to go to church—just to Sunday school, and just this once. We're having a contest."

"Yeah, well what do I get if I go?"

I told him every new kid gets a neat prize but that it has to be a surprise, knowing full well that when he discovered his treasure was a lousy pencil, I'd get beat up again. Sunday school contests made you do these things.

Sometimes we would challenge another similarly sized church in another part of the state or country. For about three or four years running, we fought hotly contested races with a church we only knew as "the Hermon Church." My friends and I thought the church must have been named after a saint we'd never heard of, which puzzled us deeply. None of our churches were named after saints. That was pretty much a Catholic or Lutheran thing, meaning it was something our churches would never do. But much later in life I learned that it was the Hermon *Avenue* Free Methodist Church in Los Angeles, which everyone in the know shortened to "the Hermon Church." As if it really mattered. Whether the church was named after saint or street, our goal was to pack more people into the pews than they did. Grown men would stand on the platform and lead cheers of "Beat Hermon," and there was even lighthearted talk of sending one of the board members out to Los Angeles to make sure they weren't cheating. By the time we were dismissed from opening exercises and headed down into our classrooms, any plans for a well-taught lesson had vaporized as teacher and students strategized over ways to trick the most unrepentant reprobates into coming to Sunday school next Sunday.

"What about Arnie?" the teacher would ask.

"Aw, he'll never come. He smokes."

"Oh my, do his parents know?"

You could almost hear our eyes rolling.

"He smokes *in the house* and they don't even care!"

Even though our church in Spring Arbor was bigger than the Hermon Church, they always seemed to beat us when it came around to the contest, so you can imagine the celebration when sometime around the fall of 1959 we beat them. Though we did not believe in dancing, any objective outsider would have thought we had backslid the Sunday we beat the Hermon Avenue Free Methodist Church. It took our pastor nearly fifteen minutes to get everyone calmed down so he could pray a long prayer of thankfulness mixed with concern for the encouragement for our competition and humility for ourselves. Still, we whooped it up all the way to our classes where I believe we were given ice cream and cookies and another break from our lesson.

It's hard to believe the same sanctuary that would be transformed into a mortuary in an hour was the scene of opening exercises. It was the one time during the week that church seemed like a pretty neat place to be. Adults who hadn't cracked a smile all week donned costumes and acted out hilarious skits. Uncle Dunk would step down off the platform and get right in front of us kids and tell us a Bible story without ever reading anything from the Bible. Sometimes they would even let us kids do things up front, like sing or recite our memory verses or pray.

One of the most amazing things that ever happened during opening exercises was when Jerri Roller would recite Scripture. Jerri was this tiny woman who was married to Gilbert Roller, who taught music across the street at the college. Like many Christian college professors at that time, they did not make much money and lived in a small house set on a tiny lot that always seemed in bloom with the flowers that Gilbert and Jerri planted together each spring.

Every now and then, Uncle Dunk would announce that next Sunday Jerri Roller would recite Scripture, and that would always be a huge draw because no one made the Bible make as much sense as Jerri did, even though she never added even a word of her own explanation. She just had this way of using her voice and her smile and her tiny little body as she leaned this way and turned that way to make the words of the old King James Version come alive, even to eight-year-olds. And we're not talking a few verses here and there, but entire chapters. Entire books of the Bible! One time she took us through the entire gospel of John, never once faltering but looking right into our hearts and repeating the apostle's account of our Lord's life on earth.

Another of the many highlights of opening exercises was the offering. I would almost bet that every church in America in the 1950s had a small, white, plastic church sitting on a little table in front of the pulpit. It was where we deposited our offering in a parade of little kids with a bunch of coins, usually wrapped tightly in one of Mom's hankies. As the piano played either "Bringing in the Sheaves" or "We're Marching to Zion," we would patiently wait our turn and then march proudly to the front, deposit the coins in a slot just behind the church steeple, and then march back to our seats. Believe it or not, the adults followed suit as well, hopefully with money that folded.

By the time we got back to our seats, enough wigglies had been worked out of our bodies so that we could sit still for a story. I realize I am biased, but I have yet to hear a storyteller who could rival any of the men or women who told us Bible stories when I was a youngster in church. Part of the reason must be sheer talent—storytelling was an art of necessity in the days without video screens and interactive devices. But a lot of credit goes to the "technology" we *did* have.

Quick quiz: name the two most common forms of visual aids in Sunday school in the 1950s. If you said Scene-o-felt and chalktalks, you are probably over forty and spent most of *your* life in church.

If you have not heard a story with a Scene-o-felt (also called flannel graphs), you have not really heard a story. A Scene-o-felt involved colorful pieces of flannel with scenes and characters from a particular Bible story oil painted on them. The storyteller would begin with a flannel-covered board about three feet by five feet, mounted on an easel. As she (Scene-o-felts were almost the exclusive territory of women) started with "One day a long time ago . . . ," she placed a bright blue flannel sky on the top half of the board, followed by a flannel sun in the corner and some billowy white flannel clouds scattered around the sky. She continued telling the story as she added a flannel meadow, a flannel shed, and a flannel tree, and then, with drama to capture a nine-year-old's attention, she would build a flannel pigpen with flannel pigs and flannel corn husks and finally, a forlorn and dirty flannel Prodigal Son.

To change scenes, she would deftly remove the pigpen and lay down a flannel path with a flannel house on the horizon and a friendly looking flannel father embracing the flannel son. To this day, I remember this parable not from my reading of it in the Bible but from Mrs. Munn's Scene-o-felt.

Like all technology, sometimes the Scene-o-felt ran into trouble. I'll never forget the time our teacher told the most moving Crucifixion story around a lavishly built flannel scene of Jesus on a flannel cross between two flannel thieves. Just as she repeated the familiar plea of Jesus to forgive those who had done this, he fell off the cross. Flannel, it seems, was subject to changes in humidity, the angle of the easel, and other factors beyond her control, but in true Sunday school fashion, she never missed a beat and actually used the mishap to artfully segue into the Resurrection.

Chalktalks were something of a more artistic version of the Scene-o-felt in that the person telling the story also had to be at least a passable artist. Where Scene-o-felters were usually women, the chalktalkers were mostly men. The concept was the same—tell a story and illustrate it at the same time, but the chalktalk had one additional feature that never failed to elicit a collective swoon from the audience. Once the picture was fully drawn and the story just about ended, the houselights would go down and with a flourish the artist would flip the switch on a little light placed just above his pad of newsprint and the colors would jump with magic. We later learned that the light was called a black light, which ironically found later use in the '70s in dorm rooms and apartments around the country.

After the story, we were dismissed to our classrooms. We kids headed nosily down into the damp basement to dark and usually cold rooms while the adults often divided up in the sanctuary, with four classes being taught at once in the four corners of the building, and for the next half-to-three-quarters of an hour the entire church studied a Bible lesson.

Our classrooms may have been without proper lighting or matching furniture, but they were the one place in church we knew we could always expect to have fun. I do not recall ever having a lousy Sunday school teacher, though that may be credited more to selective memory than reality. Perhaps there may have been an uninteresting lesson or two, but it really didn't matter because every lesson included pasting and cutting, which of course had nothing to do with computers. We're talking real paste—the white stuff that smelled so good you had to sneak a taste now and then. And real round-nosed scissors that looked just like the icons on the toolbar running across the top of your computer screen. We cut out little lambs and pasted cotton on them. We cut out stars and smeared that delicious paste on them so that the sparkles would stick. We cut out every animal that ever walked into Noah's ark, and we cut out the ark as well.

We cut big red hearts out of construction paper and pasted little doors on the front and when you opened the door, you would see Jesus, pasted to your heart.

When we weren't cutting things out of our workbooks, we colored, using fat, thick crayons that made it almost impossible to stay inside the lines. If a missionary visited, we colored the flag of the country where she served. If someone from church was in the hospital, we would make our own get-well cards and the pastor would deliver them. We made picture frames, pencil holders, wall hangings, and Nativity scenes out of Popsicle sticks, tin cans, scraps of cloth, old Christmas cards, and pipe cleaners. I am quite certain none of my teachers took instruction in interactive learning but learned early in their service to the Lord that you can stretch a five-minute lesson real far if you keep little hands busy.

One year, my Sunday school teacher was also a science teacher at the junior high school, and among other things, we learned what "likker" does to your brain when he cracked an egg into a bowl of rubbing alcohol, and we all listened to it sizzle. Do you wonder why salvation and redemption were so important to us? It's because we saw with our very eyes what happened when Jesus' blood washes your heart. First, he would show us a beaker of clear liquid and tell us that was our heart before sin entered it. Then he would pour a black liquid into the beaker and the muddiness represented what happened when we sinned. But then he would pour a red liquid into the beaker and we could see the miracle of a heart cleansed by Jesus' blood as the dark liquid mysteriously turned white.

Another year, I learned a lesson about my conscience in a manner that was so graphic that to this day I worry about mine being "rounded off." Here's how it went. First, the teacher held up a poster with a large construction-paper heart on it with a triangle next to it with one of the "points" touching the heart. The triangle was attached to the poster with a "brad," allowing the teacher to spin the triangle.

"When Satan tempts us to do something wrong, your conscience starts to spin just like this triangle, and that's why you feel something strange in your heart."

We all knew exactly what she was talking about.

"If you don't do what Satan wants you to do, your conscience stops spinning and your heart feels better. But if you go ahead and do it, the next time you are tempted, your conscience doesn't work as well."

At that point she held up another poster, this time with the triangle's "points" slightly rounded off so that they barely touched the heart.

"See, if you don't pay attention to your conscience, it spins around so much that the points wear off. If you keep letting this happen over the years, this is what happens."

She pulled up yet another poster, only on this one the triangle had worn down to a small circle, several inches from the heart. As she spun the circle, it never once came close to touching the heart. She did not have to explain what happened as each of us vowed to always listen to our consciences.

Occasionally, our teachers treated us with one of the most amazing and advanced forms of technology available to Sunday school teachers in those days: the filmstrip. Basically, this was a story captured on several frames of a long strip of film that the teacher advanced as he (lady teachers never used filmstrips) read the story from an accompanying text. There are a number of reasons why I try not to sin, but probably the most compelling deterrent to bad behavior is the filmstrip, "The Stolen Watermelon." It was a simple story that borrowed heavily from the first dramatic story in the Bible, but seeing it one frame at a time in living color left an indelible impression on me.

A mom brings home a watermelon from the fruit stand and sets it on the kitchen counter. She tells her son that she is saving it for a special meal and that he is not supposed to eat it. She leaves and he is sorely tempted. He decides he would be doing his mother a favor if he "plugged" it—cut out a small piece just to make sure it was ripe. He did that, but it tasted so good that he cut a nice big slice and ate it. And then another one. Then he realized what he had done and set about trying to get rid of the evidence. He went out behind the garage and buried what he couldn't eat. When his mom discovered the missing watermelon, she asked him if he knew where it was. He lied, and she believed him, so of course he felt awful (the points of the triangle were spinning wildly against his heart). After a few days he forgot all about it until his mother summoned him to the back of the garage where the watermelon seeds had sprouted. He confessed and was forgiven. Thanks to that filmstrip, I will never forget *or* question the Bible verse that appeared on the final frame: "Be sure your sin will find you out." (Numbers 32:23, KJV).

While Sunday school was more of a bonus for cradle churchgoers like me, it was the difference between life and death for Marv Jopling. Marv worked in a factory in Grand Rapids, Michigan, and as a young married man, he and his wife, Eleanor, went to church every Sunday until tragedy entered their lives. Their firstborn, a son, died in infancy, and soon after, Marv and Eleanor gave up on God and left the church. Over the next few years, they would have five daughters, and thanks to a local church couple who gave them rides, the girls became regular Sunday school kids. Through the influence of their Sunday school teachers and a Wednesday night kids program, every one of Marv's daughters knelt before an altar and asked Jesus to come into their hearts. Marv and Eleanor stayed home except for a couple of times a year when the girls were featured in special programs.

One weeknight, they went to a revival meeting at the church where their daughters attended Sunday school. Apparently the girls' Sunday school teachers told them that special meetings would be held to try and get more people saved, and the girls wanted so much to see their mommy and daddy saved. Marv and Eleanor accepted their daughters' and the evangelist's invitation and turned their lives over to Christ that night.

That was almost fifty years ago. Today, Marv and Eleanor are in heaven, but all five Jopling girls married wonderful Christian men who they met while they attended Christian colleges. All are active in their churches. Two of the sons-in-law are preachers as well as a grandson. On any Sunday of the year you could walk into the Sunday school rooms of a handful of churches spanning several states and find Marv and Eleanor's grandchildren teaching kids how to cut out lambs and glue cotton on them.

You will see his great-grandchildren cutting out bright red construction-paper hearts and pasting Jesus behind a little door to their hearts

Oh, by the way. David Peebles eventually visited church again, only this time the contest was for his soul, and God won. David married Uncle Dunk's daughter, and the last time I visited my home church he was singing in the choir and did not try to beat me up.

Lover's Lane

7

"It only takes a spark, to get a fire going."

ⲥⳁ

*A*s *a youngster growing up in church, my faith was pretty uncomplicated.* I was pretty certain I was a Christian, mostly because there wasn't much of an alternative. But as I entered my teenage years, adolescence brought new temptations and questions. Ironically, one of the places where I began to wonder if I really was saved was at church camp.

For me, and for most other church kids in the 1950s and '60s, camp was a blast—Sunday school times ten. Not only did it have Scene-o-felt and chalktalks, it also had crafts, mixed bathing, counselor vs. camper softball games, Lover's Lane, and faggot services.

It's not what you think.

The faggot service was the spiritual highlight of most any church camp in at least the '50s and extending into the '60s. It's anyone's guess as to why its popularity has faded. Usually held on the final night of camp with every camper and counselor standing around a huge bonfire, this solemn service got it's name from the practice of campers giving a public testimony of any spiritual victory that might have occurred at camp and then tossing a small

79

stick, or faggot, onto the flames. Okay, I guess you had to be there to appreciate it, but as a youngster, I heard of it spoken in hushed and reverent tones, as in "Rich Conley gave his testimony at the faggot service last week."

Can you imagine anyone saying that today?

There seemed to never be a shortage of people willing to participate in the faggot service because during every evening service at camp, the evangelist implored the campers to give their hearts to Jesus, even though nearly everyone at camp had done that at least once, and most of us had done it three or four times a year since we were toddlers. But that never kept the evangelist from inviting or us from accepting. Getting us saved again seemed to be the unspoken goal of camp leaders, if not the campers. It was probably a good thing to make us take our spiritual temperature so often, but for me it fostered an enduring sense that I never quite measured up.

The first few nights of camp were only marginally productive for the evangelist, as we were much more interested in finding an attractive girl from another church to walk with us down Lover's Lane.

There really wasn't an actual pathway known as Lover's Lane. Instead, there were dozens of quiet hideaways in the woods connected by a network of paths where you could take a girl and hold hands without being accosted by a counselor for PDA (public display of affection). I do not want this to get tawdry, but I must be truthful. The anticipation of knowing a certain young lady from another church had agreed to walk with you down a dark path into the woods and had also sent hints through her ladies-in-waiting that she was willing to let you hold hands with her elicited a level of sexual excitement that nearly took your breath away.

You would sit beside her during the evening service and not be the least bit affected by the evangelist's powerful stories of sin and redemption because all you could think about was her hand yielding to yours. You would bow your head during the invitation but disobey the evangelist's instruction for "every eye to be closed" as you peeked at her delicate fingers folded saintlike beneath her chin, and you ached to touch them. You would walk with her to the snack bar and be greeted by the intoxicating aroma of hamburgers and onions frying, and yet you would have no appetite because you were crazy with desire. It was almost more than you could bear—her perfume, that crisp cotton blouse with red and blue anchors embroidered on the collar, penny loafers and frilly white socks turned down at the ankle.

You would go with her to the afterglow, which would be a "singspiration." Or a Billy Graham movie that always jammed in the projector at just the worst time, making the actors sound as if they were talking underwater. Or a Bible quiz. Whatever it was, you were there only because you had to be there—it was the prerequisite for your having even the slightest chance of holding her hand. And all you could do as you sat through yet another service was calculate and project the estimated time that would be available between the end of the afterglow and curfew, when you had to be back in your dorm.

The second the afterglow was over you wanted to race out of the chapel and head for the nearest dark pathway, but instead you nonchalantly followed her out the door. As you sauntered aimlessly between the chapel and the dining hall in that parklike area glowing magically from a perimeter of light posts you realized that this was, perhaps, the most delicate moment of your mission. You were quite certain that she knew what you wanted to do, but then again, her friends might have been playing a trick on you. Maybe she had no intention of letting you hold her hand. Then again, maybe she was just waiting for you to gently reach for it and hold it as if it was the Hope

Diamond. The uncertainty only intensified your desire to find out. So you said something like, "Well, what would you like to do now?" but she always answered, "Oh, I don't care, what would you like to do?"

Why is it that girls never say what you want them to say? Something like, "Well why don't we find a nice quiet spot and just neck until curfew." But they never said that. It was always, "Oh, I don't care, what would you like to do?" You didn't want to seem too pushy or "fast," but you knew that curfew was just seventeen minutes away and you had this all-consuming urge to just grab her by the hand right then and there next to the pump house, but you dared not do it where the counselors would see it so you said something like, "Let's just walk for a while" and you hoped she knew what you really meant as you led her away from the incandescent boundaries.

I confess to a ten-beats-per-minute escalation of my pulse rate as I write this.

The first girl I ever kissed, I kissed at camp. Everyone (including the counselors), knew it was about to happen, which only made it worse. I was known as one of the slow ones. All my friends had done it, so it was time. No one believes this, but I was sixteen at the time. I had been holding hands with Nora Lee Carrier for about four days, and while it would be unfair and untrue to say the thrill was gone, my hormones were telling me I needed something more thrilling, a fact that lent credence to every sermon on sex I had ever heard. But it wasn't just my hormones. I was tired of my friends asking me each night back in the dorm, "Did you kiss her?" and having to say no, and it was so embarrassing when her girlfriends would almost scold me for not being, um, experienced. So I promised myself it would happen after the afterglow.

That night after supper I splashed a double dose of Aqua Velva on my face and picked out my cleanest shirt from the pile at the end of my cot. I brushed my teeth about six times and could not tell if the queasiness in my stomach was from nerves or the Sen-Sens I gobbled for dessert. In the brief moments between the evening service and the afterglow, I raced back to the dorm to freshen up with more AquaVelva and a quick spray of Right Guard before heading back to the chapel.

The afterglow might have been interesting—it was skit night—but all I could think of was how I was going to go through with my mission. I was an athlete and had known what it was like to feel butterflies before a big game, but this was worse. I secretly hoped it would rain so that I would have an excuse to back out, but of course it didn't, and so, after the last skit concluded I met Nora Lee at the snack bar where I bought us a Nehi Orange and grabbed two straws. We walked away from the lights and within seconds, her hand found mine, and either owing to her kindness or her own eagerness, she did not recoil, for never has there been a colder, clammier, sweatier palm than the one I offered. We strolled a little farther down the darkened path as I tried to figure out just how to proceed. Do you ask permission? Or do you just stop, lean down, and kiss? Do you keep your eyes open? If so, what do you look at? If not, what's to keep you from hitting her nose or her eyeball? If *that* happened, do you just keep trying until you land on the right spot? And if you succeed, what do you say afterwards? And why isn't my Right Guard working right now?

I think we must have circled one particular loop of Lover's Lane about six times before it became clear that this had to end some-how, and soon. Curfew was fast approaching, and I think she was a little tired of the scenery. We walked down a path where I had picked wintergreen earlier in the day, crushing it and enjoying the fresh, clean scent that smelled like toothpaste or Life Savers. I had gone there to scout out the territory and find just the right spot. Though it was dark, I knew every inch of that path.

We talked about everything, and I wondered how I would translate all of this conversation into a kiss. I mean, how do you go from camp food, or this afternoon's softball game, or last night's singspiration, or short sheeting your counselor's bed to a kiss? Finally, I realized that we had stopped talking, which was a good sign except that it made my knees weaken knowing whatever was going to happen was about to happen.

Within a few moments, we stopped walking too, and for a second I considered sprinting away. This was really a movie, and I was watching from above the treetops, and the main character was just pitiful. Slow motion. No sound. One of those frightening scenes in a horror movie. But then, she looked up into my eyes and in the moonlight seemed so pretty I almost cried. Instead, I closed my eyes and leaned toward her and somehow found her lips and for about a third of a second I could actually feel the world spinning. Only heaven could have yielded a sweeter prize.

"I love you," was all I could think to say, wishing even at that moment that I could take it back.

"Huh?" she responded.

"I really mean it," I replied, confirming to both of us that I was the stupidest person on the planet, maybe the galaxy.

Having gotten that out of the way, I paid a lot more attention to the evangelist the next night. In fact, I was a sitting duck. As good church kids, we had been given the notion that kissing outside of marriage held a prominent spot on the hierarchy of sins. Usually, the final sermon of the week focused on sin and salvation and regardless of what you had done sexually—dream about holding hands or actually holding hands—you just knew it had to be what he was talking about when he warned about the "sins of the flesh."

By Friday night, I was feeling so miserable about kissing Nora Lee Carrier on a dark path at Oak Park Camp that when the invitation was given, I was one of the first to the altar.

The preacher was a young missionary named Jim Taylor, or to be more specific, James Hudson Taylor III, great-grandson of J. Hudson Taylor who once wrote, "Do you believe that each unit of these millions has a precious soul?" and then went on to devote his life to preaching the gospel in China. In a hot, stuffy brick chapel on the grounds of Oak Park Camp in Jackson, Michigan, Young Jim, as he was often called, told us about his own work among the pagans in Taiwan—about the village sorceress who had put a curse on one of his open-air evangelistic meetings, then miraculously showed up to publicly denounce her evil spirits and accept Jesus. He reached into a cloth bag and pulled out bits of bone and hair and stone that she used to summon the demons, and we felt as we had never felt before the power of Satan.

Then he turned our world upside down by telling us we did not have to live in a pagan country to be held captive by the devil. All of us were sinners, he said. But Jesus was standing at our heart's door, knocking, knocking, knocking. Of course, every one of us kids at that youth camp came from Bible-believing, born-again-preaching churches and knew that unless we accepted Jesus we would be cast in the lake of fire when we died, and most of us had already made some kind of commitment, but on that sultry evening when I was so overcome with guilt for kissing Nora Lee Carrier, the reality of my sin came crashing down on me as never before. I joined Dennis Nowlin and Danny Newland and Joyce Kingsley and a whole bunch of others at the altar.

If I had not been saved thirteen years earlier when a thunderstorm troubled my three-year-old heart, I was that night.

But before ending the service, Young Jim had one more challenge for us: "What you have done tonight took a lot of courage. But it is all for naught if you don't share it with others. I hope before the week is over you will make a public confession of what has gone on between you and the Lord this week."

Of course, this being the last night of camp he knew what he was asking us to do. With the enthusiasm of a condemned man heading for the gas chamber, I shuffled off to the faggot service.

As the flames died down to glowing embers and a counselor's guitar strummed "It only takes a spark to keep a fire going," I faced a dilemma. Do I follow the evangelist's admonition honestly and thus indict Nora Lee Carrier who as far as anyone else knew had not yet given her lips away? Or do I hedge and confess to general fornication and risk sullying my heretofore innocent reputation?

One of the things that seemed to happen at these services was that once someone testified to a particular sin (and subsequent victory over it), those who followed—especially the guys—tended to embellish things a bit. Sort of a confessional one-upmanship. So if Dennis Scanlon admitted to swiping a candy bar from the canteen, Vic Rensberry led you to believe he was responsible for a string of breaking-and-enterings back in Dearborn, and since he *was* a city kid, you tended to believe him. By the time Marlin McMinn got done, us younger guys more or less looked up to him with the kind of awe one reserves for a sports hero.

Sometimes a counselor might try to prime the pump by calling on someone to testify, and the very possibility of this happening sent chills up our spines. While I was not present to verify the following example, I heard it repeated enough times by my brother that I can vouch for its authenticity. Apparently, one of the counselors at his youth camp called on him to "tell us what the Lord's been doing in your life," and very shortly wished he hadn't.

"Well," Bill drawled. "The Lord's been real good to me lately. So good, in fact, that one of these days I might even get saved."

By the time my turn came to throw my faggot into the fire and say a few words about what had happened to me at camp, I took the wimpy way out and sped through the most-repeated testimony of summer camps across the country in the '50s and '60s: "I love the Lord tonight and wanna go all the way with him," all the way meaning, in this case, complete commitment.

Of course, summer camp was a lot more than holding hands and Lover's Lane. In terms of appeal, however, few things matched the prospect of being away from home with members of the opposite sex. A close second, for me at least, was dorm life. For an entire week each summer, I joined a family of all boys my own age, and we pretty much did our best to break every rule posted on the registration form, which was no small task considering the way churches loved posting rules. Here's just a sample of the rules I remember:

1. No card playing
2. No talking after lights out
3. No stealing
4. No fighting
5. No swearing
6. No public displays of affection
7. No knives or matches
8. No books or magazines that do not glorify God
9. No carving names or initials on trees
10. Girls may not wear shorts
11. No tree climbing
12. No radios
13. You may not carry money at camp
14. No food in the dorms

15. Towels must be worn over bathing suits
16. You must be in your bunk during quiet time
17. You may not be in the woods alone
18. The use of tobacco or alcohol is strictly forbidden
19. Girls dorms are strictly off-limits to boys
20. You must attend all services and Bible-study classes

We pretty much used these as a checklist of things to accomplish by the end of the week, and our success depended on the counselor we got. Of all the summer camp counselors I had, two stand out. Uncle Gene was a former Marine in his mid-twenties who had a somewhat open attitude about camp rules, while Uncle Jerry took more of an inerrancy approach—if camp rules weren't in the Bible, they should have been. (I was not related to either of these counselors. At camp, every adult was either aunt or uncle).

Where Uncle Jerry paced the dorm floor for an hour after lights out to make sure no one slipped out, Uncle Gene organized after-hours excursions for his dorm (Rule #2). One night, he hiked us down a path that eventually led to a road that led to a lake where we swam in front of some unknowing vacationer's cottage. Another time he actually helped us sneak into the walk-in cooler in the kitchen for some ice cream, neatly handling Rule #3. His girlfriend (who later became his wife) was a counselor in one of the girl's dorms, so it only made sense that she let us all in for a popcorn party with the girls in her dorm (Rule #19). Being an ex-Marine, Uncle Gene referred to us as his platoon and taught us how to march and present arms. For "weapons," he showed us how to fashion coat hanger "bayonets" to the ends of branches from the trees we carved our initials in (Rule #9), which naturally required the use of his extensive knife collection. The first real switchblade I ever saw in my life was at church camp (Rule #7).

Uncle Gene was one tough hombre. Every night before lights out, he would let anyone in the dorm take a swing at him in the belly. If we didn't hit him hard enough, he'd make us hit him again. One time I took a running start, wound up, and drove my fist as hard as I could against his stomach and almost broke my hand. You think he ever had a problem with discipline?

I knew Uncle Gene was a little unusual the first year I was in his dorm. He brought along a radio but couldn't find a place to plug it in (Rule #12). These dorms were primitive setups with a single overhead light and a pull chain. No problem. Gene took a screwdriver out of his pocket, stood on a chair, unscrewed the socket, snipped the plug off the cord to his radio, and wired it directly to the line supplying electricity to the light socket . . . without shutting off the power!

Uncle Gene drove Uncle Jerry nuts, especially when he began calling him *Aunt* Jerry. But what really got under his skin was the fact that Uncle Gene's dorms always won top honors. This award went to the dorm that accumulated the most points, and points were rewarded for such things as bringing your Bible to chapel service, dorm inspections for neatness, cleaning up your table after chow time, and Scripture memorization. Despite our clandestine activities—or maybe because of them—Uncle Gene always got the best out of his campers. For example, every morning just before inspection, he helped us sweep out the concrete floor of the dorm, then sneaked over to Uncle Jerry's cabin ostensibly to ask him a question, all the while dropping a couple of candy wrappers on the ground outside Uncle Jerry's dorm. But he also taught us how to make our beds military style and insisted we practice our memory verses every night after lights out (Rule #2 again).

Uncle Gene's theological contributions were as unconventional as his support of camp rules. One of the first things he did was gather his dorm guys together the first night for a little pep talk. After telling us what we could and couldn't do and that he expected us to keep his string of "dorm of the week" awards going, he issued this directive: "I don't know how many of you are saved, but I fully expect every one of you to take care of that before you leave this week. Anyone wanna do it right now?" Believe it or not, we usually had at least one new convert step forward after his invitation.

Another time, we were talking after lights out (Rule #2, yet again) about something the evangelist had said in his sermon that a lot of us had a hard time believing. He said that it was possible for a person to never sin again if he got himself sanctified.

"What about you, Uncle Gene? Are you sanctified?"

"Of course I am," he replied as he cleaned his M–14. He was in the reserves and would be heading up north to Camp Grayling as soon as camp was over.

"You mean you don't sin anymore?"

"Not really. I mean, I might make a mistake, but I don't deliberately do bad things."

It was real quiet for a few seconds, then someone else asked what we were all thinking.

"How does that happen, Uncle Gene?"

"How does *what* happen?" He seemed annoyed.

"How does being sanctified keep you from ever sinning again?"

Uncle Gene set his rifle down and thought a minute before he spoke.

"Well, it's the Holy Ghost. If you let him, he just comes into your heart and blows all that crap out of there and makes it so clean it can never come back again."

The reason I remember it so well is that he used lots of vivid images like Draino and plungers and Roto-Rooters to nail down the concept of what a more elegant apologist might have called "eradication of the sinful nature." I am certain that Uncle Gene did not have access to *A Contemporary Wesleyan Theology, Volume One,* edited by Charles W. Carter, which, on page 267, referred to "sin that is *rooted* out of a person in crisis sanctification" (emphasis mine). It's just the way we were taught.

Uncle Gene was the first grown-up I ever heard talk so directly about sex. He told us to not ever "start doin' it with a girl" until we were married because first of all the Bible says it's a sin and also because "once you start doin' it, you can't stop." You can only imagine where our imaginations took us on *that* one. He also told us not to think we could get away with it by "using rubbers" because, he said, rubbers didn't work half the time. I can't give Uncle Gene full credit for saving my virginity until I was married, but straight talk like that made a bigger impact on me than any sermon I had heard on the subject.

Like so much of what church was becoming for me, camp gave me much but took a little in return. I really had a blast at camp, but it always came in the middle of baseball season. Missing two games never went over well with the coach, so he usually kept me on the bench for at least another game or two. I wasn't sure the fun I had at camp was worth it, but it really didn't matter because I had no choice when it came to camp.

And always, about three weeks after youth camp, I had to miss another week for Family Camp.

Church in the Woods

8

"Melt me, mold me, fill me, use me."

❧

If summer camp wasn't enough to keep me on the straight and narrow, we had an additional opportunity to experience God in the wild at something called Camp Meeting. Camp Meeting was an extension of something from a previous generation called a Brush Arbor, which, as far as I can tell, was the practice of finding a place in the woods to put up a few tents and hold church in the middle of the summer for a week or so. By the time it got to me, it was called Camp Meeting, and it involved the entire family. In fact, by the time I was a teenager, it was actually called Family Camp.

Camp Meeting was basically church camp for everyone. Our denomination owned some acreage out in the country and leased small parcels to church folk who built small clapboard shacks that were euphemistically called cabins or cottages. Those who could not afford a cabin rented an army surplus tent and lived in a tenters village for the ten days of Camp Meeting. Being sort of in between rich and poor, our family stayed in an old Spartan travel trailer that my father hauled out to a lot across the path from Vince Myers' cabin. Vince and Dave Crane were ministers who also fancied themselves as electricians and always seemed to spend most of the time at Camp Meeting on ladders trying to keep the PA system working, not an unimportant task. Every scheduled meeting, every plea for volunteers to set up tents, every notice of found car keys or lost kids was broadcast through a network of horn-shaped speakers hung from trees in the otherwise bucolic setting of Camp Meeting.

Meals were offered at the dining hall, in our case a metal Quonset building that was originally intended to serve as a military outpost in Europe during World War II. In fact, most of what the camp owned was military surplus: metal trays for eating, heavy Navy mugs for coffee, olive drab cots for sleeping in olive drab tents. Even much of what we ate was government surplus. Since my father's job was to oversee the work of all the ministers in this geographical region of our denomination, he also pretty much ran the camp. Every spring I went with him to the regional offices of the United States Department of Agriculture to load up bags of surplus food. It did something for you to see the words "For Human Consumption" on the burlap bag of cornmeal that would soon become dinner.

The camp grounds were deserted during the nine Midwestern months of fall, winter, and spring, and came slowly to life during the kids camps in the early part of the summer. But when Camp Meeting arrived, it became a small city of families serious about God. It's hard to believe, but people actually took their vacations at Family Camp, many of them dipping into their savings to pay for it or working off part of their expenses by doing dishes after each meal or cleaning restrooms. Always there was at least one family who wanted to come to Family Camp but couldn't afford it, and always someone found a way to get them there.

Each day began with an early-morning prayer meeting that, thank goodness, only the adults attended. After breakfast at the dining hall we returned to our cabins, tents, or trailers for devotions. Then it was on to Bible classes divided by ages and, in the case of adults, gender. Younger kids had their special chapels and craft buildings to keep them busy all morning, while us teenagers spent the morning in the Youth Chapel. The ladies met for three solid hours of missionary preaching in the Women's Missionary Society Building. The men seemed to get off lucky because they really didn't have anything scheduled during the morning, though to be fair, a lot of men volunteered to help teach the kids how to carve whistles out of tree branches or make acrylic paperweights.

At noon, it was back to the dining hall for either goulash, chili and cornbread, hot dogs, or macaroni and cheese, washed down with a diluted fruit drink known everywhere as "bug juice." Then it was back to your domain for another round of devotions and the much-despised "quiet time." For one solid hour we were expected to stay in our beds, presumably to allow our food to digest so that we would not get a cramp during swim time and drown. Our camp did not have a lake or a swimming pool, so we were bused ten miles to a state park, giving us maybe thirty minutes to swim and conduct two buddy checks. Then it was back to camp for a softball or volleyball game, more crafts if we needed time to finish our "bolo" ties, and then the death knell of the dinner bell, which meant that the evening service was only an hour or so away.

One of the highlights of Camp Meeting was the crowning of the youth king and queen who would then go on to Winona Lake and represent our conference at the Winona Youth Advance, a week of camp for teenagers from the entire denomination. My junior year in high school, I got nominated, which wasn't much of a surprise. I mean, my dad ran the place, I played in a trumpet trio every night in the big service, I practically lived at camp since I got back from the mission field, and this summer my older brother, Dale, was the camp youth director. It would have been hard *not* to get nominated.

The competition included a talent contest (I played "Power in the Blood" on my trumpet, with Dale accompanying me on the piano), a public interview (conducted by Dale), and an essay (evaluated by Dale). I'm not suggesting that my big brother had anything to do with my being crowned Camp King on the final night of camp, but the other guys never had a chance. My only disappointment was that my camp girlfriend that summer, Joanie Meyers, was runner-up to Sally Hawkins.

Still, Sally and I got our way paid to Winona Lake where we competed with kings and queens from all over North America. Summer romances being what they were, I immediately fell for a blonde-haired Texas girl who went on to become the queen of queens. Without Dale around to watch out for me, I finished second to a guy from Kansas. But I did win two gold medals in the hurdles in the Youth Advance Olympics and maintained a letter-writing romance for the rest of the summer; so all was not lost.

Another big deal at Camp Meeting was the annual Bible quiz competition. Free Methodist churches in our conference sent teams who had been practicing all year for this big showdown, the winner of which would also make the trek to the Nationals held in Winona Lake.

I was never much for Bible quizzing. Two skills were needed, one of which I never developed sufficiently to excel. First, you had to be able to jump out of your chair real fast as soon as you knew the answer to the question. In the early days, a judge would hold an index card just below his eyes as he watched the three quizzers from each team lined up in chairs at the front of the church. That would help him spot the quizzer who jumped up first after hearing the question, which explains the development of the "reach for the ceiling" jumping technique. Experienced Bible quizzers learned that by throwing your arms up high over your head when you jumped, you not only escaped gravity much quicker, but you also stole the judge's attention from a competitor who might have beat you but didn't reach as wildly.

By the time I joined the quiz team, an inventor devised a way to wire microswitches to the chairs that lit up a panel of lights indicating who jumped first, second, third, and so on. This new development led to a whole new technique in "jumping." Instead of going for height, you only had to get your rear end barely off the chair. So you would sit ever so lightly onto the chair, watching the panel of lights to make sure your light was off. Then, as soon as the question was asked you would barely jerk forward, releasing the pressure on the microswitch and hoping your light came on first.

I was the absolute fastest jumper on our quiz team.

Unfortunately, getting off the chair first was only half the battle, for the second skill in Bible quizzing was to know the Bible. I mean really know it. Each year, the teams were assigned a book of the Bible and any question from that book was fair game. The one year I made the team, we were quizzed over the three Peters. In my very first quiz, I was the first one off my seat for the first question:

"For twenty points, what did Peter instruct the church to do in First Peter 1:13?"

I timed my jump just right.

"Quizzer number six?"

I stepped slowly to the microphone, desperately trying to see that verse in my mind.

"Um, gird up the loins of our minds . . . be sober . . ."

I was stuck, but two out of three was never good enough.

"Ten seconds," came the droning voice of the judge.

". . . and hope for the grace that is brought unto us," I raced, just in the nick of time.

Pause.

"Incorrect. Quizzer number one."

Looking a bit too smug for my tastes, a wisp of a girl from a Detroit-area church nailed it.

"Gird up the loins of our minds, be sober, and hope to the end for the grace that is brought unto us [now looking over at me] *at the revelation of Jesus Christ!*"

"Correct!"

Still, Bible quizzing was pretty exciting. Preliminary rounds would be held during our morning meetings in the youth chapel with the finals slated for the afterglow of the Saturday night service. Teams showed up wearing custom-made uniforms and were often followed into the tabernacle by entire cheering sections from their home churches. The one year I quizzed, our uniforms consisted of black corduroy shirts that zipped open at the necks. Our quiz-team leader, Dorothy Kenney, cut out lightning bolts from bright yellow satin and sewed two of them onto the fronts of our shirts, from the shoulder to the waist so that we looked fast standing still.

Of course we won that year because Dorothy's son, Bob, was still eligible even though he had graduated from high school. Of the twenty questions, he answered seventeen, Virginia Williamson answered three, and I answered none despite being first to my feet eleven times.

I suppose I should have been disappointed, but I wasn't. Like most of what I was doing in church, quizzing had not been my choice. And I was beginning to see how different my life in church was from life in the outside world. I worked myself up into a fair amount of excitement over Bible quizzing, knowing that if my friends back on the baseball team had seen me in my lightning-bolt quiz shirt they would have died laughing. If that wasn't enough, I also knew that they just wouldn't understand what all the hoopla was about going to the altar night after night.

If the youth camp evangelist was an expert at getting pretty decent Christian kids to the altar, the Camp Meeting evangelist was his teacher. From the opening theme song, especially written for Camp Meeting, you began to feel that cardboard triangle spin against your heart. We met in an old tabernacle—a round-roofed structure with a high ceiling that was home to several families of flying squirrels. Normally, they would offer a helpful diversion but were no match for the evening services at Camp Meeting. Bev and Karyl Dunckel and Gayle Moran would sing "If You Only Knew," and then Uncle Dunk would join them later on "He Touched Me."

The missionary who was home on deputation would give a "Window on the World" each evening, and all it did was make you feel worse about your tepid faith. Here you were worried about going back to school in the fall where your friends might rib you good-naturedly about going to church while these missionaries left family and friends for four years at a time in places where being a Christian could get you killed. Usually on Saturday afternoon there would be a big missionary rally, and always the invitation was for those who felt God calling them to become missionaries. Of course, we all went forward, which is not surprising, but as I look back on some of my friends who joined me, at least six have either become full-time missionaries or served short-term assignments. I never knew for sure if I really needed to go forward because, after all, I had already been a missionary once. But somehow, hearing about people in other countries who needed someone to come tell them about Jesus touched something deep inside of us that made us answer the call.

All week long, there were plenty of opportunities for people to go forward, and sometimes the altar services would linger on into the night as the saints would gather around a weaker brother or sister who had not yet "prayed through." The altar became a battlefield where the forces of good and evil negotiated for the souls of decent men and women who had let sin smolder in a corner of their hearts. I do not ever remember our side losing one of those battles, which set the stage for the final Sunday afternoon service, the Love Feast. Love Feast had nothing to do with food but was sort of an annual report on what God had been doing in the lives of those who came to camp. It was held in the tabernacle, and like most of our Camp Meeting services, it included a fair amount of music. The leader—usually my dad—invited anyone who felt so moved to come to the microphone and share a word or two of testimony. They never kept themselves to a word or two, but it didn't matter, for these were some of the most inspiring stories a teenager could ever hope to hear. Stories about victory over temptation or the healing of a relationship or coming to faith for the first time. Stories from white-haired church ladies and strapping teenaged boys and farmers and businessmen. Sometimes a voice from the back would begin singing, and the rest of us would join in.

I will praise Him! I will praise Him!
Praise the Lamb for sinners slain;
Give Him glory all ye people,
For His blood can wash away each stain.

One of the rougher teens who had been brought to Camp Meeting by one of the pastors held us spellbound for what seemed like an hour with stories about his awful family life. By today's standards, he was describing systematic child abuse, but at the time we just thought his daddy just had a mean streak in him. Real mean. Came home drunk. Whipped him with a belt. Locked him in the basement. Busted his lip more than once. By the time he was finished, even the kitchen workers and others who didn't have to go to Love Feast were standing outside the tabernacle listening to this tragic story. He told us he came to Camp Meeting hating his daddy but gave his heart, along with his hatred, to Jesus in one of the youth meetings. He said it with such resolve that you knew he wanted to mean it, and you just prayed that when he went back home his daddy would soften up a little.

Love Feast went on for hours—sometimes continuing on through the dinner hour. Yet no one—not even the teenagers—seemed eager to leave. It was as if we were all lingering for just a bit longer, hoping that the stories we heard and the prayers that we prayed and the victories we had won at the altar would store up enough spiritual fuel to last us for another year. That was the selling point for camp. We were urged to attend—our parents were exhorted to send us—because being a Christian in an unfriendly world was so difficult. Camp promised a jolt of spiritual energy that would keep our batteries charged for the rest of the year.

Naturally, that wasn't possible, which is probably why within a few short weeks we would need yet another visit to the mountain top, and few peaks were as high as the ones we climbed during revival meetings.

9

"I was sinking deep in sin."

❧

At least twice a year, whether we needed it or not, our church had a revival meeting. Usually, we needed it.

Revival meetings were sort of like regular church on a sugar high. One solid week of church every night, with a heavy emphasis on altar calls. It was a time when we were encouraged to bring our "unchurched friends" to church so they could get saved, but more often than not most of the regulars got saved all over again during the revival.

I had wanted to avoid theological and doctrinal issues, but given what I just said about getting saved again, perhaps a word or two about the nature of salvation is in order. When it came to getting saved, there were two camps among the "Bible-believing churches" of my youth. The Baptists and other churches that looked to John Calvin as their doctrinal ancestor, believed that once you got saved, you were saved for life. Nothing you did could get you unsaved. Actually, they also believed that nothing you did could really get you saved in the first place because only the "elect," or those whom God had already chosen to save, could actually get saved. They even used the word "irresistible" to describe what happened once God decided to save you. You couldn't say no, and you couldn't change your mind later and go back to being unsaved. They called this eternal security.

My church, on the other hand, was part of a group that looked to the Anglican circuit rider, John Wesley, who taught that salvation was a little more iffy. First of all, you had to decide you wanted to get saved in the first place—it wasn't something God had already decided specifically for you by name—and then you had to decide almost daily to *stay* saved. God gave you the freedom, we believed, to turn away from him, a condition we called "backsliding." If you died during a time when you had backslid, you would go straight to hell. My Baptists friends called this eternal *in*security, which was actually pretty accurate.

I remember envying my Baptist friends because they could do pretty much whatever they wanted to do and not lose their salvation, while I, on the other hand, had to get saved all over again if I committed a sin, which was often. I used to joke that we Wesleyans got our salvation the old-fashioned way: we earned it. But in my growing up years it wasn't a joke.

You would think there wouldn't be much of a market for revival in a Baptist church, since once you got the whole church saved it was pointless to have altar calls every night for a week. But actually, they had as many revivals as we did; probably more. When I asked a Baptist preacher friend about this he explained that while they didn't believe in backsliding (as we did), nonetheless they felt that a person who was "away from the Lord" needed to renew that relationship. They called this a "recommitment." So technically, they didn't get saved again. But he also explained that in case a sinner came in who was one of the elect, the revival meeting would be as good a place as any to close the deal, so to speak.

That's the beauty of the revival meeting. Regardless of what you believed about salvation, revivals served a great purpose. Mostly, they gave us all a chance to think deeply about our relationship to Jesus and then do something about it if we thought something needed to be done. And the universal place for that to be done was at the altar. Everything about the revival meeting was aimed at getting us to that long wooden bench at the front of the church where we could do serious business with God, and few things got you started in that direction better than the music. We actually had "song evangelists," men who had this special gift of "song leading" that coaxed the high notes out of you and whose wives almost always played the "revival time" piano, which consisted of a lot of cascading arpeggios that left you almost weak by the time you finished the song.

Imagine being fifteen years old. You're trying your best to live a godly life in a pagan high school. You hear guys like Tom Comeau and Pat Farley swear and tell dirty jokes, and the sun shined mighty brightly on them. You, on the other hand, go to church and don't smoke or go to parties, and you still get C's in math and never get the cool girls to notice you. And just that day Brenda Evans asked you why you didn't "peg" your pants, knowing full well that your mom wouldn't let you because tight pants were worldly. You come home after football practice to tuna casserole and your mom's reminder that tonight is the first night of the revival, and so you arrive at church feeling lower than a snake's belly and within three minutes after finding your seat with the rest of the youth group, the entire church erupts in:

I serve a risen Savior, he's in the world today.
I know that he is living, whatever men may say.
I see his hand of mercy, I hear his voice of cheer.

And just at this moment in your life when you needed something—some reminder that you were not alone on this journey to a place you couldn't see led by a man you knew only from a very long book with thin pages and strange language . . .

He's always near.

You are on your way back up the mountain, and the next song only makes the path seem easier:

I know not why God's wondrous grace
   To me he hath made known,
Nor why, unworthy, Christ in love
   Redeemed me for his own.

The more you sang, the better you felt about your faith. Let all your buddies trade old copies of *Playboy* magazine and make fun of you for going to church. It didn't matter because . . .

I have decided to follow Jesus,
I have decided to follow Jesus,
I have decided to follow Jesus,
No turning back, no turning back.

So what if you couldn't go to movies or play cards or dance? What difference did it make if you missed a pick-up game of basketball on a Sunday. It was the price you paid for a greater reward.

When we all get to heaven,
   What a day of rejoicing that will be.
When we all see Jesus,
   We'll sing and shout the victory!

If the song evangelist was any good, he would always make us actually shout the word "shout" on that one, just as he always made us hold the word "lives" until we almost passed out on the final chorus of "He Lives."

Still, there was this nagging sense that your life didn't quite match up to the song, which set the stage for the sermon, and the preaching at a revival was unlike the sermons you heard at regular church. My dad once explained to a group of ministers the difference between evangelistic preaching and expository preaching. Expository preaching was more like teaching, and it was reserved primarily for Sunday mornings. Its purpose was pretty much to help people understand the Bible and apply it to their daily lives, though sometimes, especially when it came to the Old Testament, you found precious few of us who got the connection between, say, Naboth's vineyard and junior high school. Expository preachers knew Greek and Hebrew and could tell you the context of the particular passage they had selected, along with what various scholars had said about it.

A really good expository preacher could open the Bible, pick a selection, and just walk you through it almost word by word, and here's where the Baptists had it all over us Free Methodists. Give a Baptist preacher a Bible and a pulpit and he can even make the genealogies make sense. Probably the best expository preacher I ever heard was Bert Westenberg, who also happened to be my wife's pastor before she was my wife. This guy would just sit back during the early part of the service and let his assistants handle the music and announcements and offering—the little stuff. But almost before the soloist sat down, he was on that pulpit like a tiger, paging through a big old *Scofield Chain Reference* with pages that looked like used Kleenex. He'd have you on Mount Sinai and then back in camp with the Israelites so that you could almost smell animal sacrifices and see the golden calf right before your eyes, even though all you ever really saw was Bert standing in front of that fake stained glass that Baptist churches used so much.

Evangelistic preaching, on the other hand, was more persuasive. Although it still used the Bible, it was more story driven than expository preaching, and always, the story was always the same:

John 3:16. This was the very first Bible verse most of us memorized, and it sums up the text of every evangelistic sermon ever preached. Of course, evangelistic preachers used other biblical stories, the most common being the Prodigal Son, the Rich Young Ruler, Saul's conversion, and Jesus' in-your-face advice to Nicodemus: you must be born again.

But where the evangelist really earned his stripes was in the telling of his own stories. As much as I disliked going to church every night during the week of revival meetings, it was hard *not* to pay attention. I'd get all settled into a nice daydream and then get pulled away from it by the power of the evangelist's stories. He started kind of low key, telling us about the man who was a drunkard who beat his wife, and then found a gospel tract on the floor of the factory where he worked and knelt right there to accept Jesus and returned home a model father and husband. Then he moved on to the soldier who was not a Christian but kept a New Testament in his shirt pocket anyway and one day in battle took a shell right to the heart but lived to tell about it because the bullet only went partly through the Scriptures, miraculously landing right on John 3:16! Of course, each story took about fifteen minutes to tell, spun with great detail and drama. I never fully believed all of them, but they got my attention. Finally, he closed with a powerful story about a teenager who grew up in a Christian home and then rebelled and got a girl pregnant and lived for the devil for years. He never married the girl but stayed in touch with the boy. One day the little boy was taken to Sunday school by neighbors and met Jesus. He prayed for his daddy to get saved every night. When his daddy would visit the little boy would plead, "Please let Jesus come into your heart, Daddy." But Daddy never responded. He went off to war and never came back.

You can't *not* listen to these stories, and when you hear them you can't avoid wondering about your own spiritual condition, which was the whole purpose of revival meetings.

After about forty-five minutes of stories—each one outdoing the last, the preacher got down to business by closing his Bible. When an evangelist closed his Bible you knew that the only thing standing between you and eternity was the invitation, for as he folded the leather cover between his hands, the organist soundlessly slipped out of her pew and took her place at the keyboard, and halfway through his next sentence the soft and lonesome strains of a familiar tune settled over the sanctuary like a mother's hand stroking her baby's curls.

Just as I am without one plea
But that thy blood was shed for me.

"I'm going to ask you to stand, and I want every head bowed and every eye closed." To this day, when I hear those words my hands get sweaty, and I can feel my heart beating in my throat.

"Now with every head bowed and every eye closed, I want to ask you to do something. I know there's at least one person in this sanctuary who has strayed from the Lord. Maybe it's a Mom or Dad who has lost the joy of the Lord. Maybe it's one of our young people who's done some things lately that haven't honored the Lord Jesus Christ."

How could he have possibly known that about me?

"I know it can be a struggle trying to walk the straight and narrow and that when you stray off the path it may seem like you'll never get back where you belong. So I'd like to pray for you tonight, whoever you are. Just lift your hand so I can see it, and in a moment I'll pray that the Lord will give you victory."

I confess. I left one eye just barely open as I tipped my head from one side to the other, trying to see who raised their hands. Even as I did it, I knew it was wrong, and that was yet another convicting reason for me to go ahead and raise mine.

"Yes, I see that hand. And that one. Yes. Yes. Hold them up high so I can see them. Oh, there's going to be a celebration in heaven tonight."

As I peeked around, I saw maybe only one or two hands go up, which made me wonder if the evangelist had double vision or something. But then I realized there were probably lots of people in the back rows with their hands up.

It didn't really matter how many hands went up, though. The most important hand in the whole place was mine, and try as I might, I could not keep from quickly raising it and pulling it back down to my side—as if the duration with which it was in the air was in direct proportion to the severity of my sin. But even as I slipped my hand up, I knew I was trapped, for no evangelist ever stopped there. Ever.

"Now as Brother Jim comes and leads us in a verse or two of this song, I'd like all of you who raised your hands to step out of your aisles and come kneel at this altar. We won't tarry long, so come quickly."

It worked every time. Well, sort of.

Sometimes, only a few—or even no one—went forward, even after four verses of "Just As I Am." That's when the invitation became a spiritual battle, or at least a battle of the wills. The evangelist would tap the song leader on the shoulder, who would back away from the pulpit to let him give it another try just as we finished singing, ". . . oh Lamb of God I come."

"You know, the devil would like nothing more than for me to close with a word of prayer and send you all home, but I can't do that and call myself a minister of the Gospel. I *know* there's at least one person in this sanctuary who can feel Jesus knocking at his heart's door, so we're going to sing another hymn, and I want all the saints to pray for that one person to step out and receive eternal life."

Even as he was speaking, the organist deftly modulated from "Just As I Am" to one of the most persuasive invitational songs ever written:

Softly and tenderly Jesus is calling,
Calling for you and for me
See on the portals he's waiting and watching,
Watching for you and for me.

When I was about fifteen years old and a revival meeting was approaching, I took a serious spiritual inventory and tried to clean up every sin that I knew about, such was my dread of having to respond to an altar call. I listed every sin I could think of and knelt by my bed at night and prayed as earnestly as I could, confessing those sins to Jesus and asking him to forgive me, not so much because I wanted forgiveness but because I did not want to come under conviction when the invitation was given at next week's revival. Just once I wanted to sit through "I Surrender All" knowing that I'd already done it.

In addition to the two revivals we would have at church— spring and fall—we usually had yet another opportunity to get saved at a community-wide revival. Because my dad was often in on the planning of these events, I learned an awful lot about ecumenism. Basically, there was precious little of it among Bible-believing churches in the '60s.

First of all, there was the question of who would participate. Catholics were definitely out, largely because we weren't sure if they even believed in getting saved but also because we knew if the

Catholics were invited, the Baptists wouldn't come. Then there were the Lutherans, and here again, some extraordinary doctrinal footwork was necessary. The Missouri-Synod Lutherans were quite conservative theologically and, therefore, closest to the kinds of churches that wanted to put on revival meetings. But they pretty much kept to themselves, believing that they could only worship with churches with which they had entered a formal communion, which meant other Missouri-Synod Lutherans. The "other" Lutherans—now known as the Evangelical Lutheran Church in America—probably would have helped out but, because they were thought of as "liberal," were seldom asked. Even thirty years ago the Methodists were confused about what they believed, so generally, they did not join these community-wide revival meetings. Presbyterians in those days were generally conservative enough theologically to get along with the rest of us, but a revival meeting just wasn't their style. While we might get an occasional Presbyterian to show up, as a church they didn't support revival meetings. That pretty much left it up to the Baptists, Salvation Army, Nazarenes, Wesleyans, Evangelical Free Church, Assemblies of God, Church of God (Anderson, Indiana, not Cleveland, Tennessee), Missionary Church, Evangelical United Brethren, Free Will Baptists (really!), Bible churches, and Free Methodists, and there's where the *real* hurdle to ecumenism occurred: what to do about the unchurched who got saved. In other words, to which church would a seeking convert be recommended? The fear was that if the revival produced a hundred new Christians, would they all be sent to First Baptist (which seemed unfair) or spread equally among the participating churches (which seemed unfair to First Baptist)?

There were other issues. Some churches didn't believe in the use of musical instruments. Others wondered what to do if a woman showed up sleeveless. The Assemblies usually pressed for a healing service toward the end of the week, but the dispensationalists usually prevailed. The Baptists believed as soon as someone got saved he should be baptized, but others thought that was giving the Baptists an edge.

Somehow, these and other disagreements got worked out, and for one week, Christians from a dozen or so churches in the area experienced the closest thing to unity as one could expect this side of glory.

Our revival meetings were carefully planned events, but *real* revival was a spontaneous moving of God. It was not announced with handbills or posters, nor did it always wait to happen in church. In my lifetime, I have only experienced a true revival once, and it was a very scary thing to behold.

I had graduated from high school and was attending Spring Arbor College, across the street from my church. We were gathered in the college auditorium for the required chapel service. The guest speaker was from Asbury College, a similar small Christian college in Wilmore, Kentucky. He very calmly told about some strange things that were happening back at his campus. Unlike most other chapel services, no one was writing letters or doing their homework. In fact, it got eerily quiet.

He finished speaking and sat down behind the pulpit, which normally signaled the end of the chapel service. But before anyone dismissed us, a student walked to the platform and began confessing to some pretty remarkable sins. Then one of my professors did the same thing, followed by another one. The next student at the microphone said that he had spread lies about another student. He named the student and right then and there asked for forgiveness. The two met at the altar and hugged each other for the longest time, and by now there was a long line of students and faculty waiting to speak. Occasionally, someone would lead out in a hymn, and there would rise from this body of students a great harmony of praise, and then more testimonies. Classes were canceled, meals were missed, others who had skipped chapel joined us, and this service which began at 10:00 in the morning continued throughout the entire night and into the next day. Carloads of students were dispatched to other Christian college campuses into what has since become known as "the Asbury revival."

I have read that when John Wesley rode into a town and began conducting meetings, the impact on local culture was immediate and widespread. Taverns closed for lack of business. Prostitution suffered from a lack of customers as well as transformed providers of services. Truants returned to school, church attendance rose, and crime fell. On a smaller scale, similar changes were noticed at our Christian college. On the outskirts of our "dry" village was a business establishment called the Pony Bar. On occasion, some of us would sneak out there for a sample from their menu, so to speak. But when the Asbury revival hit our campus, those after-dark excursions ceased to the point that when I saw one of the "regulars" in town, he remarked that the owners were thinking about turning it into a legitimate restaurant to reclaim some of the lost business.

The sad thing about these genuine movements of the Holy Spirit is our temptation to do them ourselves. Evangelical Christians have *always* struggled with humanism—taking things into our own hands because we really do think we could do them just a little better than God could. The best, or maybe worst, example of this is the way we take a good story and try to make it better, which is why annually almost more conversions are reported than there are people in the world and why the supernatural has apparently become natural in some circles. It would be unkind to question the authenticity of those who seem to be whipping us all into a Holy

Ghost frenzy—I truly believe their intentions are pure and their devotion unblemished—but I must confess to being a bit skeptical whenever I hear reports of revival breaking out.

Even in the case of the Asbury revival, there were excesses that should not be attributed to the spirit of God. One evening when someone got up and reported that on the fourth floor of Ormston Hall there were a handful of guys who had not yet repented and were even at that moment drinking Ripple from paper cups in one of the dorm rooms. Before we knew it, he had organized a parade of zealous students to march around the dorm chanting "Repent! Repent!" which did not seem to have the desired effect on the reprobates upstairs. To this day there are preachers who are still trying to keep the Asbury revival alive.

I would not want this critiqued by a really smart theologian, but I think God views revival as kind of a messy, inefficient way to do business. True, he does it now and then, and it is a wonderful thing when it happens, but I don't think he likes doing it that way. From what I have read, he seems to be a lot more personal, enjoying the one-on-one approach instead of having to disrupt the general nature of things that he created in the first place. He can do that, and it certainly doesn't hurt to pray for it to happen, but in between those wonderful, scary, massive movements of his spirit, I think he takes more joy watching us work alongside him.

In the '60s we called it witnessing, and if you know anything about it you understand why we would much prefer a revival as the best way to get our friends saved.

Winning Souls

10

*"Everybody ought to know,
Who Jesus is"*

გი

As *a youngster in Japan, telling others about Jesus seemed like a per-*
fectly natural thing to do, but when I entered high school, it lost
some of its appeal. Actually, it lost most of its appeal. But that's what
we were constantly being told to do. Witness. The Great Commis-
sion. Soul winning. Share your faith. Tell them that they needed
Jesus. Lead them to the Lord.

No matter what the preacher called it, we didn't want to do it.

I was sixteen years old when I went on my first "witnessing
weekend." Our church youth group had just had a special speaker
for a week-long emphasis on sharing our faith with our non-
Christian friends, and to wrap things up he invited us to come back
to church on Saturday morning to practice what we had learned.
I did not want to go, because I had heard from the older kids what
we were in for.

"They're gonna make you go door-to-door," Barry said.
"They'll take you to a new subdivision and drop you off, and you'll
have about twenty houses to hit, and everyone will think you're
selling something and tell you to get lost."

But I had to go. Whenever the church had something for us kids, our parents always made us go. There were only about two people who could get away with not going, and they were Rodney Phipps and Jerry Crandall. They were also the kids at whose homes we could play cards, and I was sure there was a connection there.

Anyway, the speaker lived up to his advance billing. He told us the gospel was the most precious gift we could give anyone, but he also told us most people didn't want it. Then he told us they were lost without it and that if we really cared about their souls we would not hesitate to devote a weekend to telling others about Jesus. He told us it was the least we could do.

Easy for him to say, I thought. He was paid to tell others about Jesus, though it seemed as if he always did it at church. I'd like to see *him* come to Western Junior High School and try to talk to kids about Jesus. Bucky Evans, the first kid I ever heard use a four letter word that began with the letter "f," would have had this guy for lunch.

But he just kept on telling us that even though we would be "persecuted" (at least I could agree with him there), we *had* to be willing to risk everything for the sake of the gospel. "What if no one had told *you* about Jesus?" he asked.

That line of reasoning had sort of a delayed effect on me. I mean, come on. An *American* who had never heard about Jesus. The notion of me not ever knowing about Jesus just didn't register. Every one of us kids in youth group had known about Jesus forever. We could not think of a time in our lives when we *hadn't* known about Jesus. But then he would drive home the clincher: "Do you realize that for some of your classmates, the only time they ever hear the name of Jesus is when their parents take His precious name in vain?"

I reluctantly had to admit he was probably right, because once, at a Little League game, I heard Skip Jenkins' mamma, who was our coach, chew out an umpire, starting with "Jeez, ump," and we all knew that Jeez was just a syllable away from the name of our Savior. Skip didn't go to church as far as I knew, and it was likely that Jeez was the closest thing he knew about Jesus.

I signed up to be at the church at 8:00 sharp on Saturday morning.

Sure enough, after the hot chocolate and donuts, the evangelism expert announced that we would be dropped off at a subdivision where we would have a certain number of houses to visit. He gave us packets of information that included a brochure entitled "What We Believe," a church bulletin for services the next day, and a gospel of John. He told us to ring the doorbell and, when someone answered, introduce ourselves, tell them what church we were from, hand them the material, invite them to church, and then ask them if they knew where they were going to spend eternity.

Now imagine yourself at 9:00 on a chilly Saturday morning. You just got up, put on your robe, and were about to settle into your favorite chair with a cup of coffee and the morning newspaper when this sixteen-year-old kid is at your door asking you about eternity. I knew our leader hoped that most of them would answer, "Well, Jeez, I haven't thought much about eternity. Come on in and tell me all about it," but no one ever invited me in to present the plan of salvation. Almost to a person, however, these unsuspecting hosts were gracious and kind and usually just politely thanked us, took our material, and said they would think about it.

I'm certainly not knocking door-to-door evangelism. A few years ago I worked for a Christian magazine, and one of my assignments was to interview Dr. D. James Kennedy, the founder of an evangelism program known as Evangelism Explosion. It is highly successful and relies almost totally on going door-to-door to ask people about their relationship with Christ. I returned home from his Florida headquarters on a cold, rainy night and settled into my easy chair with the newspaper and a cup of coffee when there came a knocking at my door. My wife answered it and invited a group of four people into our living room. As soon as they started, I knew what they were selling: Evangelism Explosion. Just for fun, I let them go through their pitch, and when they came to the part where they asked me if I knew where I would spend eternity, I couldn't resist.

"You guys are from Evangelism Explosion aren't you?" I asked.

"Well, um, yes, but how did you know?"

"I just got back from a meeting with Dr. Kennedy, and you know what? He would be extremely proud of you."

We had a great evening celebrating our common faith, and believe it or not, I began attending their church, College Church of Wheaton, Illinois, based solely on the winsome yet direct manner in which they were reaching their neighborhood with the gospel.

Not every method of witnessing was as straightforward. All through high school, my locker partner was a very nice girl named Sue Cook. One day, in our sophomore year, we met at our lockers as we usually did in the morning, but this time I noticed she was wearing a little pin on her collar that was simply a question mark. It wasn't exactly jewelry, but more along the lines of a campaign button. Like an idiot, I took the bait.

"Hey Sue, what's that pin for?"

"I'm glad you asked, Lyn. It represents the most important question any of us can answer," she politely responded.

Not bad, I thought, as I instantly recognized what was going on. Sue was from a church that was even more strict than mine.

She explained that the most important question we could ever answer was whether or not we would let Jesus into our hearts.

"Aw, come on, Sue. You know I already know that."

"Yeah," she smiled. "But I just wanted to practice on you."

A few weeks later, I noticed a really cool-looking bronze pin on my dad's dresser. It was not unusual for businessmen to wear little pins on their lapels that either represented a fraternity or service club like Kiwanis or Rotary, but this one was a little different. It simply spelled out the letters C-I-T-A.

I asked my dad what it meant, and he said that the letters were an acronym for "Christ Is The Answer." He told me that he wore it to Kiwanis Club and to the YMCA, where he played volleyball at noon, and that if another guy asked him about it, he had a great opportunity to share his faith.

Unlike the cheesy question-mark pin, this little bronze accessory looked classy. If there was one thing I was learning we Christians didn't have, it was class. The high school I attended was a "consolidated" school, meaning it brought together kids from three or four small towns. Spring Arbor was pretty much totally Christianized, but Parma and Woodville had plenty of pagans, or at least that was what we were told. It always seemed as if the kids from those towns had the nicest cars, the nicest clothes, and that even when we did something as important as telling others about Jesus, we usually did it with the subtlety of an Amway salesman.

Something inside told me I had to wear that CITA pin, so without telling my dad, I swiped it and wore it to school the next day. I sort of hoped that Sue Cook would notice it so I could show her I was just as outreach-minded as she, but if she saw it, she never said anything about it. I went to my first-hour class, and again, no one noticed the pin that could have led them into a personal relationship with Jesus Christ. In fact, not one person noticed my CITA pin until I went to football practice, where I learned a cardinal rule of witnessing: never try to share your faith in a boy's locker room.

I was a little late and walked in as most of the guys were just slipping into their pads.

"Hey Cryderman, teacher make you stay after school?"

Laughter and ribbing.

"Or was it Mary who made you stay after school?"

More laughter, along with some jokes and comments that I cannot repeat. Then, Marv Allen, a guy who went about 280 and played left tackle spotted my pin. "What the hell does *kyta* mean?" he bellowed, eyeing my pin as he hooked up the straps on his shoulder pads.

The locker room got real quiet, giving me the perfect opportunity to say a word on behalf of my precious Savior. I was something of a leader on the team, and before me stood at least ten bona fide pagans. Great guys, but clearly outside of the family. None of them went to church, which, in a way, made me envy them, but at the same time I sorta felt sorry for them. And I really did care about their souls, or I should say I had been taught to care about their souls. Normally, I didn't think about their souls but sometimes at night just before I went to sleep I thought about what might happen if one of my pagan buddies died, and what I remember thinking about most was that if they died without accepting Jesus into their hearts, they would surely go to hell *and their eternal punishment would be all my fault.* That is how we were taught when it came to witnessing.

We were also taught to be ready to speak a word on behalf of our Lord because you would never know when He might provide an opportunity to witness. Finally, my CITA pin worked. Thanks to Marv's irreverent question, the door to salvation had opened wide, and all I had to do was explain what that little pin meant. These guys were like brothers. They blocked for me. Did battle in the trenches while as a running back I got all the glory. I really wanted to see them get saved and have their lives turned around, but I froze. I could not get the words out. I had even practiced my response for such a time as this: "Those letters stand for a little phrase, 'Christ Is The Answer,' and what that means is that if we believe in Jesus and turn our lives over to him, he will help us find the answers to all our problems."

But for some reason, I could not say those words. I saw them written down in the back of my *Moody's Christian Workers New Testament*, and I felt them in my heart, but I could not say them.

"Aw, I think it's Spanish for something. I just found it on my dad's dresser."

I felt like Peter when the rooster crowed for the third time, and I felt even worse a few years later when I learned that Marv was killed in an explosion.

You would think failures like that strengthened my resolve to spread the gospel of Christ clear through my high school, but I actually got worse. By the time I was a senior, the worst sinner in the school could have come up to me and asked, "What must I do to be saved?" and I probably would have mumbled something and walked away.

Like most teenagers of my generation who had spent their lives in church, I was beginning to become ashamed of the faith that I had been given. Part of this had to do with the ways we were encouraged to witness. In addition to the stealth approach that used buttons and gimmicks to trick people into asking about Jesus, we used what would now probably be called "the geek method" of evangelism. That is, our leaders seemed to stay up late devising evangelistic techniques that made Christian kids look like idiots.

One summer between my junior and senior years in high school, our youth group leader announced that we would go to a local resort area and witness. Naturally, he got our parents involved, which meant we had no choice but to sign up. He picked a Sunday afternoon because he knew that was when the largest number of pagans would be at the beach, and because he knew there wasn't much else we could do anyway, it being Sunday and all. If you can visualize this one witnessing event, you will have a fairly representative picture of the way a lot of us were forced to win the world for Christ in the '60s.

Families and groups of young people are swimming and sunbathing and tossing beach balls around in a park by the lake when a church bus shows up and out rolls thirty or so kids still in their Sunday-go-to-church clothes. We could not wear bathing suits because we did not believe in swimming on Sunday, and we kept our Sunday clothes on because we were ambassadors of Christ. We gathered in a corner of the park a few yards away from the sandy beach.

Talk about embarrassed. We arranged ourselves two deep in a semicircle facing the beach. I thought about the college students who spoke at our youth group one Sunday about the time they went to Florida over spring break with Campus Crusade for Christ. They said that they too were embarrassed and almost backed out a number of times but stuck with it and saw dozens of hungover kids get saved. So when our leader gave us the cue for the first song, I swallowed my nervousness and started singing.

Between songs we would take turns giving our testimonies, and I must say, we were better than I thought we would be. Our youth group leader insisted that we write out a testimony and then memorize it. He said that way we would be able to project better and deliver it in a way that impressed the audience. By this time a few curious onlookers wandered over and, to their credit, politely listened and even applauded after each of our songs. After our testimonies, our leader invited any who had questions about Jesus Christ to stick around and "we'll be happy to talk with you."

Up to that point, I was feeling pretty good about getting through this ordeal. But having to mingle with others and talk to them one-on-one about Christianity made my blood run cold. Like so many other times, I just couldn't do it. We had been told to walk around the beach after our "concert," prepared to lead anyone to Christ who would rather get saved than swim, but as far as I could tell, no one seemed eager to deal with some guy wearing a white shirt and carrying a Bible.

I looked out over the tangle of tan bodies splashing in the water and wondered why anyone would want what I had. And to be perfectly honest, I wanted what they had: the chance to go swimming on a Sunday without sneaking out to do it. Even though I could be easily spotted in my white shirt and tie, no one came up to me and asked how to get saved. In fact, I secretly hoped no one would ever get saved at these things because that would only encourage our youth group leader to do it again. That is a horrible thought for a Christian to think, and I don't know whether to blame our leaders for *making* us do such foolish things for the gospel or myself for not being willing to *do* something foolish for the gospel.

I was always afraid to witness because I could never find a way to talk about my faith that seemed natural. Either the technique of the day seemed like a setup that any clearheaded pagan could detect from the first gimmicky question or the very vocabulary of faith seemed so foreign to the world in which I lived that what witnessing I did could best be described as halfhearted. If I was forced to give my testimony, I could say the words as well as anyone. But my heart just wasn't in it. Except for the time I got a call from my neighbor.

I was eighteen years old and living at home for the summer, working at a tire factory to earn money for college. My parents traveled quite a bit on church work, so my younger brother and I basically had the place to ourselves. It was pretty late this one night, and I was just about to go to bed when the phone rang.

"Lyn, could you come over?" It was Brenda, the next-door neighbor. "Larry's acting really strange, and I think he just needs to talk with someone."

Larry had been the branch manager of our little bank and was one of those guys everybody loved. They were relatively new to the community and had moved into the house next to my parents' home. This was the first home in my entire life that was not a parsonage. My father had been elected to our denomination's highest office, a post that did not include a parsonage. In the old days we would have had to move back to Winona Lake, but now they let the bishops live wherever they wanted to. I suppose it put a bit of a financial strain on a man approaching retirement to have to buy a house, but if so, he never complained. Nor did my mom. In fact, she was relieved. When they picked out their house, it was in a subdivision about three miles outside the little village where I grew up and around the corner from my best friend, Bob Crist. The neighbors were wonderful people, but not many of them went to church, which was sort of a blessing to my mom. "Now I can work in my garden in Bermuda shorts!" What she meant was that she no longer had to worry about what the church people might think to see the pastor's wife in shorts.

Anyway, it was not long after Larry moved in that it became apparent he had a drinking problem. He was never belligerent or mean, and he seemed to be a pretty good husband and father. It was just that once he got home from work, he was always about half-lit. He'd laugh a little too easily, and his eyes had that glaze that comes from a little more than an evening cocktail or glass of beer. I later learned that on the way home from the bank, Larry picked up a six-pack and finished two beers—twenty-four ounces in three miles. And once he got home, he kept opening bottles until he fell asleep on the couch.

One day, in one of those backyard conversations, Larry casually mentioned that he was no longer managing the bank but was, instead, a cook at a restaurant in a nearby city. It seemed odd at the time that he would quit such a position of responsibility for what amounted to a short-order cook's job, but later I learned that he didn't quit the bank job. He was fired for returning from lunch too many times a little tipsy.

"What do you mean when you say he's acting strange, Brenda?" By then I knew about Larry's drinking, and the thought of spending the rest of the evening trying to sober up a drunk was about as appealing to me as, well, going to church.

"I dunno." I could tell Brenda was both worried and angry. "He's blubbering like a baby and lying on the floor and all, but he won't tell me what's wrong. He really likes you so I asked him if he wanted you to come over and he said he did."

Great, I thought, but told her I'd be right there.

When I got to the side door, Brenda let me in, and I headed down the basement steps as she hollered down, "Larry, Lyn's here." Then she closed the door to the basement behind me, which made me feel sort of trapped and more than a little afraid. I'm eighteen, Larry is in his early forties, and this was during one of those periods when you could say I was not exactly in the center of God's will. In fact, a few weeks earlier I played softball on Sunday and broke my finger. My mother reminded me that the Lord lets things like that happen when we disobey God and to this day, I have an index finger that won't bend as proof.

Larry was on his knees in front of the sofa and sort of slouched over. You could tell that he had been crying, and it was also pretty

LYN CRYDERMAN

obvious that he'd had a few. I didn't know what to do, so I just
kneeled down beside him and asked him what the trouble was.

"I'm a total failure, Lyn, and I hate it that you have to see me
this way."

"You're not a *total* failure," I answered, realizing I should have
dropped the word *total*.

And then he started crying.

He sobbed that he was ashamed of himself for telling me dirty
jokes, me being a preacher's kid and all, and that sort of got me
because now I felt like maybe *I* was to blame for Larry feeling so
awful. But it was true. Every now and then he would see me out
in the backyard and walk over and tell me the funniest dirty jokes,
and even though I knew I shouldn't laugh, I couldn't help myself.
In fact, I used to look forward to him sauntering over because I
knew he always had a few good jokes for me. And now he was on
his knees in his basement in the middle of the night, feeling like a
failure because he told me some dirty jokes.

Then he told me that he was ashamed of himself for losing his
bank job and that it looked like he was about to lose his job at the
restaurant. He went on about how much he looked up to my dad
and that he felt lousy about corrupting me and that he was really
trying to be good but was really a lowlife, and I'm just kneeling there
wondering what to do when it hit me. This may be the one time
when the only thing I could offer was my faith, weak as it was.

"Um, Larry, none of us is perfect," I started, groping for the right
words.

"I mean, we go to church and all, but that doesn't make us better than anyone else. In fact, even though I go to church a lot, half
the time I think I'm the worst sinner around."

Larry kind of looked up as if I'd just told him one of his own
jokes.

128

"You gotta be kidding. Your dad is about the most perfect man I ever met, and you guys are all just super. And look at me. I'm nothing but a dumb drunk."

I told him that being a Christian had nothing to do with being perfect, a fact that I wasn't all together convinced of myself, but this wasn't the time or place to work through *my* problems.

"You can be just like my dad if you tell God you're sorry and invite him into your heart." I could hardly believe what I was saying.

"How do I do it?" he asked.

I was too much of a church lifer to not recognize the similarity of his question to the one asked by the Rich Young Ruler: What must I do to be saved?

I told him to just follow along as I led him, phrase-by-phrase through a prayer that I had heard many times before: "Jesus, I am a sinner. I am sorry for my sins. I invite you into my heart, and I will try to live for you from now on."

It seemed to work. Larry calmed down, and even though it sounds corny, you could just feel a quiet peace fall over the room. Brenda had been listening, and she came over and gave Larry a big hug and then hugged me too, and then I left.

I would like to tell you that Larry got his bank job back and is now the president of the entire chain, but within a year, Brenda and the kids left him. He was working in a restaurant in Florida when he died. From what I gather, Larry never won the battle against the bottle.

Will I see Larry in heaven? I wonder a lot about that, just as I wonder if I will see the thousands of Japanese who also prayed the sinner's prayer some forty years ago. It would be easy to place Larry's conversion in the same category as a jailhouse or foxhole conversion, and he is certainly not the first drunk who turned to God in an alcohol-induced moment of shame. On the other hand, someone could say my own conversion was artificially induced by an evangelist who played on my own guilt to show me that without God I too am a failure.

What I know for sure about this inglorious effort at evangelism is that somehow all those witnessing weekends and share-your-faith seminars culminated in my being able to explain the gospel to someone who was lost. The lapel pins, the tracts, the gimmicks— they all may have been a little contrived and silly, but they reinforced within me the most important news we have to share: Jesus saves.

What seems foolish to us may be the work of a Master who knows how to take water and turn it into wine.

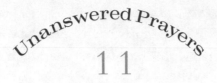

11

*"While on others thou art calling,
do not pass me by."*

ε✧ᴐ

I do not ever recall not believing in God, but as I approached adulthood there was a lot about church that led me to stray from the faith I had been given at an early age. Like most church kids of the '60s, my rebellion was pretty mild. Other kids my age were burning American flags and dancing buck naked at rock concerts and taking any drug they could get their hands on. So sneaking out to a movie might seem pretty tame, but if you grew up in a conservative evangelical church like I did, it was bordering on heresy. It would probably make a better story to suggest that my decision to go to a movie was an act of principled defiance—a deliberate challenge to all I had been taught about how a Christian is supposed to behave in the world. It wasn't. I simply had never in my life been inside a movie *the-AY-ter,* and it just seemed as if it was time to see what it was like.

I was eighteen years old.

Movies were never much of a temptation to me when I was a youngster because everyone in our town went to the same church, which forbade its members this particular form of entertainment.

So this was one prohibition that was unaccompanied by peer pressure. Even if I *had* wanted to go to a movie, the closest theater was fifteen miles away. While we may not have agreed with our church's view of movies, it was not very high up on the hierarchy of forbidden things we wanted to do.

But when I entered junior high school, we left the safety of Spring Arbor and were bused to a "consolidated" school where kids from several communities attended. For the first time, we rubbed shoulders with other kids who did not have the same religious upbringing as we did. Some had no religious upbringing at all, and it was here that I began to understand just how different I was from the rest of the world. It was also here that movies became a sore spot for me. One of the regular Monday morning topics of discussion as we waited for classes to start was which movie we had seen over the weekend. I dreaded having one of my new pagan friends ask me what movie I had gone to.

"Um, I didn't get to the theater this weekend," I mumbled, then tried to nudge the conversation to another topic.

I felt horrible, not because I told the truth but because I knew my telling of the truth left a false impression, and that was the way a lot of us handled our discomfort with being different. Legally truthful, but always dancing along the border of a lie. I always felt as if I was caught between convictions I did not hold and compromise, which I did not enjoy.

Up until now, church had been benign. A harmless mixture of boredom and amusement. Now it began to feel like a liability. When my friends finally asked my why I never seemed to go to movies, I wanted to tell the truth and say, "Because I go to this stupid church that teaches it's a sin to go to movies, that's why!" But I loved the church so much that I lied and said things like I didn't like movies or I didn't have time or I'd rather play football, and, of course, they knew all along the real reason. You could only give so many phony excuses before they caught on, and then you had to endure the ridicule that followed once they knew you weren't allowed to go to movies.

When my eighth-grade class went on a field trip to a local theater to see a rendition of *Romeo and Juliet,* I was one of about six students who had to stay behind.

I tried to reason with my father along the lines of how it shouldn't be so bad to go to a good, clean movie like the ones that Walt Disney served up in those days, but that line of reasoning never worked. The dollar I spent on *Old Yeller* was supporting the movie *business,* which to him was a vile and scurrilous enterprise. That sort of made sense to me except that once a year he would pack the family into the sedan and drive us to the old Music Hall in Detroit to see "Cinerama," which even though it was sort of a glorified travelogue, it was still a movie as far as I was concerned. Weren't those dollars also going to Hollywood to help make *Never on a Sunday* or *In the Heat of the Night?*

Dad was pretty rigid on this, but he wasn't as bad as some. A lot of people hated movies so much that they prohibited the use of *celluloid* in church. That meant *any* kind of movie, including those released each year by World Wide Films, the evangelistic film division of the Billy Graham Evangelistic Association. A great after-church activity on Sunday nights was the showing of a Billy Graham film in a large church where area youth groups converged, but we could always count on a few churches to boycott it.

To be fair, I have to admit that as a parent, I wish there was an artful way to prevent my kids from seeing not only a lot of movies they have seen but much of what they have seen on television as well. My father may have been overly legalistic about this, but he and many like him were sincere in their concern for the kinds of things that were pumped into our minds in the tantalizing fashion that only film can deliver. And he has been consistent. Now in his eighties, he has never been inside a movie theater, and I would be the last person to try and convince him he's missed something significant.

But I was certain I *was* missing something so I decided to go to a movie. Not wanting to directly challenge this prohibition, however, I went incognito. Despite it being July and one of those sultry nights where you would sweat standing still, I donned a hooded sweatshirt and pulled the hood up over my head as I stood in line at the Capitol Theater on Michigan Avenue, the main drag in the city where everyone in our town shopped. Just up the street was Field's department store, and across from the theater was Woolworth's. It would not be out of the question for someone from my church—even my parents—to be out shopping, so I wore the hood to make sure they wouldn't see me standing on the sidewalk waiting to get into the Capitol Theater.

Once inside, I shed the sweatshirt as I nervously negotiated the foreign territory of a theater lobby, only to run into our Sunday school superintendent. Evidently he, too, wanted to see John Wayne in *Hellfighters*. He gave me one of those looks that said, "I won't tell if you won't tell," and without saying a word we headed for our seats.

Now here is one of those ironies that convinces me that God has a streak of mischief in him. *Hellfighters* is a movie based on the life and adventures of a man named Red Adair, who was famous for being able to put out oil-well fires. Whenever a well caught fire, whether it was in his native Texas or halfway around the world, they called Red Adair. Just two years before the release of this movie, geologists discovered a rich deposit of crude oil about twenty miles west of our little village, and drilling began almost immediately. Excitement spread as the oil flowed, and a lot of poor farmers got rich fast. But then a well caught fire, sending flames hundreds of feet in the air. If you looked into the western sky at night, you could see the glow from the fire twenty miles away, and on at least a couple of occasions, my dad drove us over to the site so we could see it firsthand. Being an old newspaper photographer, this oil-well fire put him and a lot of volunteer firemen in hog heaven.

After several weeks of local fire departments struggling with the blazing oil well, they finally admitted defeat. It was just too much for them. Guess who they called to put it out? Red Adair.

My dad would have loved *Hellfighters*.

Just as we were warned, though, this one small act of rebellion led me down a slippery slope that, if not sin and perdition, was at least as guilt producing. The next thing to go was the Sabbath. But here again, it would be a stretch to suggest I set out to challenge the teaching of my church. I totally accepted the view that Sundays ought to be different, and that God's decision to rest on the Sabbath was instructive. I just thought we had a pretty narrow idea about what constituted rest and that if one day of the week should be fun, it ought to be the day we called the Lord's Day.

So after church one Sunday I picked up my girlfriend, and we drove to Lake Michigan. I had packed a little charcoal grill and some steaks and we found a nice little spot along Lake Michigan to have a little picnic. Not exactly an unholy act, except that we took our bathing suits along and fully intended to take a dip at the beach, which would have been okay for Mary, since she was a United Methodist, but was borderline heresy for me.

"How about a nice steak?" I asked as I pulled my little 1968 Opel Kadette into a secluded picnic area.

"Sounds great!" She could hardly believe that this guy who never did anything on Sunday was suave enough to broil steaks.

I set up the little portable grill next to the picnic table and poured the charcoal into it. Then I splashed some lighter fluid on it. I had never broiled anything before but had watched my dad enough to get the hang of it. Or so I thought.

After a few minutes, the flames died down. I squeezed some more fluid on the charcoal and lit it with a big "whompf!" But again, after a couple of minutes, no fire.

"How are the steaks coming?" asked Mary who had slipped into her bathing suit in the ladies rest room and was lying on a towel working on her tan.

"They'll be ready in no time," I answered bravely as yet a new round of flames sputtered out.

Once again, I squirted more lighter fluid on the pile of briquettes and lit it. As the flames flew high, I set the picnic table with the paper plates I had brought, along with a bag of chips and a Thermos of lemonade. I even thought to bring along a vase from under the kitchen sink and some flowers from my mom's garden.

When I checked on the fire, however, the charcoal was as black as night and almost as cold.

"Hey, I'm getting hungry. Need any help?" I think she knew I was having a little trouble, but I was enough of a guy keep her away from the fire.

"Naw, I never like to cook my steaks too fast. Makes 'em tough."

As if I really knew. All I wanted was to get the lousy fire going and hear those steaks sizzle. So I poured enough fluid onto the charcoal to incinerate a small shopping center and threw the steaks onto the grill. They sizzled for a while, and when the flames died down, I fed more fuel to the fire.

That seemed to work, so I continued that pattern for the next several minutes until I could announce with pride, "Come and get it!"

She was polite, but I tasted the meat too. If you have ever eaten rubber soaked in kerosene, you know what our steaks were like. They were blackened before it was considered a chic culinary technique, only just beneath the crusty surface, the meat was bright red. Neither of us finished our food, despite having not eaten for five hours.

In all the anticipation of our romantic meal by the beach, we hadn't noticed the clouds rolling in. Almost on cue, it started raining just as we were telling each other we weren't that hungry. So much for my plans for a romantic walk along the beach.

Mary was a good sport as we sat inside the steamy Opel and listened to the Association on my eight track. I had it all cued up to "our" song—"Along Came Mary"—hoping to resurrect a little mood. Somehow, it wasn't working. Maybe it was the charcoal in my teeth. Or the fact that we were both starved. Or that we were in an imported car with a gear shift and parking break lever between us.

With a very kind but weary smile, she leaned over and said those words every guy hates to hear: "Maybe we better be heading back."

On the way home I got pulled over because one of my headlights was out. But since I didn't have my registration with me, the trooper wrote me a ticket. Whatever romance was lingering inside the Opel vanished as I drove back onto I–94. By the time I pulled into her driveway on Church Street in Parma, Michigan, it was clear to both of us that she could do much, much better. Within a week she returned my senior picture and my graduation-cap tassel. She would have returned my class ring, except I never had one because we didn't believe in jewelry.

I tried to dismiss this tragedy as lousy planning on my part, but a nagging voice aided by that spinning triangle next to my heart assured me that this is what you get for breaking the Sabbath. You might think I'm crazy for attributing a lousy Sunday outing to disobedience, but then you weren't with me several Sundays later when I decided to go fishing. On this occasion of flaunting my

Lord's-day upbringing, the symbolism of what happened should have convinced me to never do anything but go to church on Sunday and play *Sorry* or take a nap in the afternoon.

I packed my fishing pole and tackle box into the backseat of my Opel and headed for one of my favorite spots along the railroad tracks separating two lakes known collectively as Lime Lake. The routine called for me to walk east along the tracks and then take a little trail south along the shoreline of the larger of the two lakes. I got to my spot and set my tackle box on the ground. When I reached down a moment or two later to open it and select a lure, a large snake had slithered across the handle and, at that very moment, reared up to strike. I took off running, and it actually chased me. Finally, I turned on it, hoping to either scare it away or maybe stomp on it, and the thing reared up and bit me on my thigh. Now a blue racer is not venomous, and the bite didn't get through my blue jeans. But it did not take a Bible scholar to figure out why that snake impeded my access to the tackle box and then bit me in a final exclamation mark to the Sixth Commandment.

I don't want to belabor this, but just about anytime I have played a sport on a Sunday, I have sustained an injury. I have had concussions, broken bones, sprained ankles, and various other mishaps when playing ball on Sunday. Intellectually, I knew that God had better things to do than trip me as I rounded third base, but as a young adult beginning to question some of what I had been taught in a lifetime in church, waiting for an X ray in a hospital emergency room induced a fair amount of soul searching.

At the same time, I began to question the benefits of this faith of mine. What kind of God would take away a girl as wonderful as Mary Roberts? Why would he send a snake to bite me just because I was out enjoying something as harmless and benign as fishing? And what could he possibly gain from sending me to the emergency room in the middle of a backyard football game? Is Sunday *that* big of a deal to him?

Dancing was next, but to be truthful, this was never a huge temptation except for the fact that it was a major prohibition in our church. We used to joke that our church did not believe in premarital sex because it might lead to dancing. It was not a real funny joke considering the number of hasty marriages in our church youth group.

The only times I wished I could go to dances were the homecoming dances and the prom. Can you imagine being a starter on the football team and dating a cheerleader and *not* going to the homecoming dance? Our youth group leaders, bless their hearts, tried to organize alternatives to the dances, usually calling them "the fifth quarter." But sitting in someone's living room and eating popcorn and playing charades was a lousy substitute for what was going on back at the high school cafeteria.

So I sneaked out to a dance after a football game one Friday night, but all I did was sit on the sidelines and watch everyone else have fun. Somehow I thought that if word got back to my parents that I was at the dance, I could truthfully admit that I might have *gone* to the dance, but I didn't *dance* at the dance. Legalism opens you up to all sorts of ways to weasel out of trouble.

But the main reason I didn't actually dance was that I didn't have the slightest idea what to do on the dance floor. This was the era of the Frug, the Shing-A-Ling, the Watusi, the Mashed Potato, the Boogaloo, and the Swim, and none of them looked like something I could do. Sometimes, when no one was home, I would turn the hi-fi up real loud on WIBM 1450 and try to dance to the Temptations, Supremes, Paul Revere and the Raiders, or the Monkees, and watch my reflection in the big picture window across the living room from the fireplace. What I saw embarrassed me so much that I usually was able to fight off the urge to sneak out to a dance on Friday night.

If you are thinking that sneaking out to dances and movies and fishing on Sunday constitute a pretty mild rebellion, you are right. I don't recall loud arguments or me storming out of the house yelling back something like, "That does it! I'm gonna go see a movie and you can't stop me." And I can't say that breaking these rules opened the door to more serious things. By the time I was comfortably settled into a Christian college, the troika of drugs, sex, and rock-and-roll hit our campus as they did every other campus, Christian or secular. For some reason that I still do not fully understand, I was never tempted by marijuana, which was then and still appears to be the gateway into more dangerous pharmaceuticals.

Sex, of course, was always on our minds, and, despite the restrictions of segregated dorms and heavily enforced curfews, it was more than just a mental exercise. It is probably shameful of me to note this, but one of the most prevalent confessions during the Asbury revival involved tearful girls who admitted that they had violated their own standards of purity. There was, of course, much squirming by many of the guys for fear that names might be mentioned, and it is a tribute to the honor of those girls that confidence was kept. But even with a temptation as powerful as sex in a culture of free love, I somehow managed to maintain my own standards, or at least the standards that I was taught in church.

So as not to leave the impression that I was an ascetic who spent most of his time in cold showers, I should admit that on several occasions I did my best to keep up with the spirit of the age, but in some uncanny fashion I was always foiled in my attempts. An RA would knock on the door, giving me just enough time to sneak out the ground-floor window. An off-campus apartment became available for the night, but one of us would chicken out. A carload of us would drive to Michigan State University where a party promised pleasures beyond our imaginations, but by the time we got there the conversation turned political, and the next thing we knew, we were making posters for an antiwar march.

My mother would attribute those interventions to angels, and I would not disagree.

While I struggled with these fairly normal temptations to a kid who grew up in church, the real battle was against the more forbidden forces of questions and doubt. I suppose one could say of any era that it appears God was either powerless or disinterested, but during a period when we murdered a president and his brother, put a man on the moon, sent 58,000 of our young men to die in a jungle, marched in the streets while "the whole world is watching," made love with the one we were with, turned our military against black people and students, most of what I was taught seemed up for grabs. Or to put it another way, the things that really seemed to matter to the church in which I was raised—dancing, card playing, and movies—did not seem to matter much to the world in which I was living.

For example, when it came time for me to register for the draft, I had heard that it was possible to classify yourself as a conscientious objector (CO) but that your chances of having your local draft board approve that status for you were much better if you could show that your church or synagogue supported this view as a matter of their religious teaching. I went to my pastor to ask him about this, partly because I didn't want to go to Vietnam but also because I was curious about what my church had to say about war. For the first time in a long time, I was genuinely interested in what my church believed.

My pastor told me that he did not think I should classify myself as a CO because that's not what the church taught. He told me that

Christians have always answered their government's call to defend the land, and while he did not come right out and say it was my duty as a Christian to take my chances with the draft, he pretty much convinced me to forget about becoming a CO, which I did.

But then a few months later, I went to an antiwar protest at the University of Michigan, about thirty miles east of our campus. There were a lot of groups who had set up booths along the perimeter of the Quad, and I picked up all the printed information they were handing out. When I got back home, I started reading through the leaflets and came across one that listed all the denominations that officially supported members who wanted to declare themselves conscious objectors. And right there alongside the Mennonites and Quakers and other Anabaptist churches was the Free Methodist Church.

Dancing did not seem all that important anymore.

Up until now, I had only been embarrassed about my church. I was smart enough to realize that the silly rules they enforced did not have anything to do with the real message of the Bible, though there were times when I wasn't sure. One time I asked my youth leader why we couldn't play cards or go to movies, and he pretty much admitted that there wasn't anything in the Bible about those things, but then he threw in the argument that always worked on me. He said that if I, as a Christian, was seen at a dance, I would be a "stumbling block" to others. Those weren't his words. They came straight from the Bible (1 Corinthians 8:9), which still carried a lot of weight for me. The last thing I wanted to do was make it hard for anyone to be a Christian.

But then I got to thinking how this argument was even sillier than the rules themselves. Did we really think guys like Dave Cline and Mike Shore stood inside the cafeteria where we held our dances, just waiting to see if I walked in?

"Hey, Mike, isn't that Lyn Cryderman out there dancing?"

"Sure looks like him to me."

"That does it then. I'm never giving my heart to Jesus."

"Me either."

There was a certain arrogance and cultural naiveté to think that the rest of the world took their cues from the extremely small number of us who defined our faith by what we didn't do. Most of what the Bible says about the way our actions speak for our faith focuses on what we *do*—things like giving food to people who are hungry and giving them clothes if they don't have any and the one we had the hardest time with—being decent to other Christians.

If anything, our prohibitions were the real stumbling block to others. Who in their right minds would have wanted to join a group of people who not only did not appear to have much fun but were always fighting other people who went to church.

Still, I could have probably lived with the legalism because I knew most clubs had rules that outsiders seldom understood. But I was having a hard time understanding how my church could withhold information that at least would have given me a spiritual context for understanding why I was so uncomfortable with this war that was dividing our country. I cannot say that I would have filed for conscientious-objector status had my pastor told me the truth. But the incident plunged me into a period of deep suspicion regarding just about everything I had been taught.

It would be tempting here to suggest I was some kind of serious philosophical seeker of higher truth. A rebel with a cause. In fact, most of my generation gets a little too much credit for altruism—as if we were the only generation that wanted to make the world a better place. True, we were the peace-and-love generation, but like all college students, we also did not need much of an excuse to get crazy. Woodstock was more of a party than a statement, and much of my quest for meaning in life was, quite honestly, more selfish than socially redeeming. To put it another way, I didn't start going to movies because I wanted to make a statement of protest against my church's social mores. I basically just wanted to see a movie. My friends were getting high and getting laid not so much because they wanted to change the world but because they wanted to have a good time.

But the process of testing some of what I had been taught raised a lot of other more important questions.

For example, every year our church raised thousands of dollars for missions. Missionaries from Africa or Latin America would come and show slides of really poor people coming to their clinics or worshiping in ramshackle churches, and we would get all teary as we reached for our wallets. It always made me pretty proud of our church for its concern for the world, and I would probably still think nothing of it had it not been for Newton Ambuyo.

Newton was the chief of one of the largest tribes in Kenya, and somehow he came to our college as a student, along with his brother, Hudson, who was an Olympic silver-medallist boxer. Despite being prominent leaders in their tribe, they were poor, and I probably do not know all the details, but the way they helped pay their tuition was to clean the restrooms in the dorm! I too had to work off some of my school bill, but my job was to sit behind the desk in the game room, handing out Ping-Pong paddles when it didn't interfere with my homework.

I wasn't honorable enough to go to my boss and ask him to let Newton and I switch jobs, but deep inside I thought it was more than an accident that a white boy with good connections got a cushy job while a black guy, despite being a tribal chief and an Olympic medallist, got the dirty work.

Even *that* might have been understandable except that one day I was asked to take a group of prospective students on a tour of the campus. Two of the students were African-Americans. After showing them the field house and the dining commons and the classrooms, one of the black students got smart with me.

"Don't you guys have any janitors here?"

Puzzled, I assured him we did but asked him why he wanted to know.

"Because I haven't seen any black people yet."

He knew exactly what was going on, even if he never knew anything about Chief Newton Ambuyo.

To be fair, when the riots of 1967 burned down most of Detroit's 12th Street corridor, our college president discovered that along with their homes, many young black men also lost their chance to go to college. Whatever money their parents had went to rebuilding their houses. So the college sent a recruiter to the neighborhood and offered twelve scholarships right on the spot.

It was a noble and Christian thing to do, but it showed us all how little we understood the gulf that separated black and white in America, even in Christian America. For starters, no one gave much thought to the fact that one of the first thing a guy does when he goes to college is check out the girls. Can you imagine the uproar when twelve black guys arrived in our village and started looking at our white girls? Can you imagine a major donor getting word that his daughter was dating not just a *Nee-grow*, but one from the 'hood?

We tried hard, and so did they, but by the end of the year, ten of the twelve surrendered and went home.

During this tumultuous period, hardly a week went by without some kind of protest, usually involving a march or sit-in. It did not escape my notice that ministers often were at the front lines of these demonstrations. But not my ministers. We *did* have a sociology professor who not only participated in some of these protests but broke ranks with the rest of the faculty and began attending a multiracial church in a nearby city. But he was pretty much dismissed as a kook.

When I asked why my church never took a stand against the war or asked us to go to Selma and march with the Civil Rights Movement, I was told that it was unwise to mix our faith with politics. That the church should always transcend politics and just be the church. That once a minister took a political position from the pulpit, he had compromised his high calling.

It made sense to me, and as a student leader on my college campus, I used that very argument to reign in those who wanted to burn the American flag in chapel. The only problem with this line of reasoning was that practically every church leader I knew was telling their congregations to vote for Richard Milhous Nixon.

Yet I hung in there. I reasoned that politics was kind of the mirror image to legalism. Neither were essential to the gospel. I held on to my faith by cheating on the rules and privately siding with the liberals who took to the streets, but I was beginning to feel miserable. I wanted an authentic faith—one that would allow me to be who I really was, not who others wanted me to be. I wanted to stay in the church in which I had spent my entire life, but it looked so different, so foreign. Always before it had seemed like the one place where I belonged, but now I felt as if those wonderful saints who were smiling at me had their fingers crossed behind their backs. I wasn't sure they would hold me if I fell, and most of the time I felt as if I were falling.

The unraveling of my faith was accompanied by incidents that called into question a lot of what I had been taught about God. One of those incidents involved the anticipated healing of Sherry Hudberg. Sherry was one of the most talented musicians on campus, wholly devoted to serving God. She was preparing to be a missionary and spent most weekends ministering in area churches. If anyone had the spirit of Christ, it was Sherry. Except that she was blind.

When word got out that there would be a healing service for Sherry, I was skeptical. I did not doubt that God *could* heal. I just had little hope that he *would*. Our church was not one of the dispensationalist denominations who taught that God pretty much got out of the healing business after the apostolic period. In fact, in the early days you would find a small bottle of oil in the pulpits of every one of our churches, ready to be used for anointing should anyone asked to be healed. And I had heard many marvelous stories of tumors disappearing or pain vanishing after a healing service. I had just never seen such things with my own eyes.

I felt convicted, however, that my skepticism might "quench the spirit" in Sherry's case, so I began praying in earnest that Sherry would be healed. I even fasted one entire day, praying several times throughout the day for Sherry to regain her sight.

We gathered in a small auditorium, about a hundred of us kneeling around Sherry. One of the campus ministers talked to us about healing, reading from that passage that says if our faith is the size of a mustard seed it was enough to move a mountain. We expected a mountain to be moved that day.

It wasn't.

Several of us prayed out loud, and then the minister laid his hands on Sherry's upturned head. I fully expected for her to open her eyes at the end of the prayer and shout. I wanted to be close to her to see how she would react when she saw her friends' faces for the first time.

To her credit, she did say that for the first time in her life she was able to see a light, ever so briefly. But when she left that chapel, it was with her red and white cane tapping to and fro to show her the way, just as she entered.

We all took it evangelistically. We told ourselves that maybe the real healing took place inside each of us, but the only thing I felt inside was utter disappointment. We told ourselves that God, in His great wisdom and sovereignty, knew that Sherri would be more of a blessing to others in her blindness, but I didn't like the picture of God that created for me.

In fact, I was not liking a lot of what I was seeing. Uncle Gene wasn't the only one in our church who taught that once you got filled with the Holy Spirit you would never sin again. It was one of those bedrock doctrines of our denomination. Most of the altar services I witnessed included several dear saints struggling with the fact that even though they thought they were sanctified, they had committed a sin that week. Since I knew so many of the ministers who prayed with these old ladies, urging them to yield even *more* of their wills to the Spirit, I began to resent them because I knew *they* weren't perfect either.

The more I wrestled with these imperfections in my church, the more I began to see myself in the mirror. And I didn't look any better than the church that had begun to disappoint me. Somewhere along the way, I had learned that you can't hold someone else to a standard you're unwilling to reach yourself. How could I blame the church for doing what I did all the time: put on a good outward appearance to hide what was really going on inside?

There is a small hill south of Spring Arbor overlooking a marsh behind our house on Harmony Road. I used to hunt rabbits and pheasants there, but on a dreary afternoon in the spring of 1968, I hiked through the marsh and up hill to an old apple tree and climbed up onto a low-hanging branch. From my perch I could pretty much see the steeple of the church poking above Art Crandall's place on Main Street. I thought about all the times I had sat through sermons. I recalled revival meetings where I had felt the pull of the spirit and once again tried to find the victory that was promised. And I took stock of what all of that religious activity had actually done for me.

Despite a lifetime in church, I could not honestly lay claim to the kind of faith I sang so robustly about on Sunday morning. So I quit singing.

I climbed down out of the tree, slogged back through the swamp, crossed my backyard, and shot baskets in the driveway until it was dark.

Lost and Found

12

"From the waters lifted me,
now safe am I."

~

Even though I was living at home while attending college, my parents were pretty good about letting me make my own decisions about how I would live my life. While I didn't declare outright that I would not be going to church anymore, I basically quit going. I just couldn't stand to be around people who seemed to have all the answers, when the only real faith question I had was not whether there was a God but whether I even cared if there was or not.

When summer rolled around after my freshman year in college, I started working at the Goodyear Tire and Rubber plant in Jackson. The money was good, plus a generous overtime policy allowed me to work on Sundays, which helped keep church at bay. The monotony of loading tires into railroad boxcars gave me plenty of time to think about what I believed, but matters of faith were not on my mind as I raced to the parking lot one Friday afternoon in June. I had met Audrey, a girl at college who had invited me to visit her in Toronto whenever I could get away from work that summer. I called her earlier in the week to see if the offer still stood (it did) and then arranged with my supervisor to get the weekend off.

This was going to be one of those weekends your mother warned you about, and I couldn't wait to leave.

My day started at 6:00 A.M. and included eight hours of throwing truck tires around at the factory. The six hours of driving flew by as I anticipated all that awaited me in Toronto. Unencumbered by any conscious claim to faith, I was ready to experience just about everything that had been denied me by my church.

I hit the city limits just as the sun was setting and could hardly contain my eagerness as I left the highway and began winding through neighborhoods with the directions I had scribbled on a sheet of paper guiding me. Almost to the minute when I said I would arrive, I found Audrey's house.

I also found that she was with another guy and just never bothered to tell me but said it would be okay if I went out to eat with them, which just about made me puke. But what else was there to do?

I crawled into the back seat of his little Volkswagen, and we drove to a small restaurant near her house. I ate dinner with them, feeling very much like the odd man out. Then he insisted they show me the city, as if I drove all that way for a Greyline tour. So for another two hours he drove us all around Toronto, pointing out landmarks interspersed with conversation that told me more than I cared to know about him. I discovered that he was a youth pastor studying at a seminary in Toronto and that one day he hoped to be a senior pastor or a missionary. From the way he glommed all over her, it was apparent they were pretty serious about each other and about God. Not exactly what I had in mind when I left the factory.

We got back to her place around midnight, and I was thinking he would leave and I would spend the night there, but they had other plans. I was to follow him out to his parents' house and spend the night there. I tried every tactful way I could think of to get out of it, but he insisted. So for what seemed like an hour, we wound around the suburbs and then out into the countryside north of Toronto and pulled up to a comfortable-looking tri-level in the middle of nowhere. By now I just wanted to go to sleep and then maybe hook up with Audrey the next day and try to figure out what happened.

We went up to his bedroom, which had an extra bed that would be mine for the night, and within minutes I was under the covers. He asked if I minded if he kept his light on for a while, and I mumbled that it would be fine with me, assuming that he wanted to read a little. Earlier in the evening he got all excited telling me about a youth camp where he would be speaking the next weekend, so maybe he was preparing one of his talks.

I was just about to fall asleep when he propositioned me.

He must have sensed the mixture of fear and disgust that made me instantly feel as if I was about to drown.

"You don't have to if you don't want to."

I couldn't speak. I was practically paralyzed.

He started talking really fast, but I wasn't listening. I ran from the room and into the bathroom across the hall and threw up.

A woman's voice called out, "Douglas, is that you?" I was in such a panic that I could not think straight. I had no idea where I was or how to get back to the highway, and I did not want to go back into that room.

"It's okay, Mom. I have a friend staying over, and I don't think he feels too good. G'night, Mom."

"Good night, dear."

It was surreal.

When I went back into the bedroom, the light was still on, and he was sitting in bed reading his Bible. I went over to the side of his bed and got my face real close to his and threatened to scream at the top of my lungs if he didn't draw me a map to show me how to get back to Highway 401.

I think I must have looked pretty scary because he jumped right up and got out a sheet of paper from his desk and drew me a map. He asked me if I wanted him to make me a snack before I left, and I told him to forget it. I also told him he was sick and that he better tell his pastor about his problem because if he didn't, I was going to, which of course I never did. I just got in my car and started winding my way back to the highway, feeling scared and dirty and very, very lonesome.

By the time I got back to the highway, I had been up for more than twenty hours and was starting to nod off. I pulled off at a truck stop to buy a bottle of NoDoz and started chewing them down to help keep me awake. Then about an hour outside of Toronto, I began to fall apart. The empty blackness enveloping my little Opel served as a poignant reminder of just how alone I was. It was a tunnel without any light at the end—just two weak beams reaching into the abyss. About every five minutes I would slam my hand against the steering wheel and curse my horrible luck. After being a pretty good boy all my life, I decided to do something pretty bad, and *this* happens. I needed someone to blame, and after I finished with Audrey, only one person was left. The God whom I had abandoned was in for one last earful from me.

I started yelling at him as I tried to keep the car between the lines on Highway 401. I told him that this is what he got for letting me get set up so badly. I asked him how he could let somebody like that become a youth pastor. I asked him if he knew what was in store for some of those young boys at the youth retreat next weekend. I told him this was why I had quit going to his church. That as far as I could tell, everyone who claimed to be his follower was a phony and that the least he could do is leave me alone. I screamed a lot more horrible stuff at him until just west of London, Ontario, it hit me.

He took it.

It wouldn't have taken a lot of his supernatural power to send me headfirst into an overpass since I had swallowed so much Benzedrine and was already dodging all sorts of things flying across the road. I had never really talked to God like that and couldn't believe I was getting away with it.

I gave in. It might have been the drug, the lack of sleep, or the emotional trauma of being propositioned by the boyfriend of the girl I had driven six hours to visit, or it might have been the Holy Spirit. Whatever it was, I dropped my fists and opened my heart and admitted defeat. The God I tried to escape was all I had and I knew it. He wasn't a church or a set of rules or a tradition. For me, at that particular moment, he was my Savior.

My little white Opel Kadette became a confessional booth.

I had always envied my Catholic friends. They could go inside a little box and tell someone all the bad things they had done and walk out lighter than when they entered. It seemed as if at that moment I couldn't carry my guilt any further, so I just started leveling with God. I didn't bother with the movies or the card playing or sneaking out to the Pony Bar not just because it didn't seem important anymore, but because I figured he knew all that anyway. Instead, for the first time I spoke my doubts out loud. I told him I really wondered if everything I had been taught about him was true. I told him I wasn't absolutely certain that when I got saved I really meant it, and that I wasn't sure anyone could know for sure if they meant it or if they were just playing the best odds. I told him that practically all of my prayers had gone unanswered and that most of the answered prayers I had heard about had never been verified but were waved around like trophies at a prizefight.

LYN CRYDERMAN

I told him that I doubted whether he was even listening and that if he was he must be pretty stupid because there were a lot more important things going on in the world than a strung-out kid on his way home from a rotten weekend.

And then I pretty much ran out of things to say to him.

I have heard people whom I respect say things like, "God told me" or "God said to me," and I must be honest and tell you that I had never heard God say anything to me. Not a word. But on that awful night in the car after being up for more than twenty hours and popping NoDoz and screaming at God, I heard him for the first time in my life. It was not an audible voice or words spelled out in red letters in front of me or anything spooky like that. I did not see a vision or feel his hand on my shoulder, nor did his words from the Bible suddenly come to mind.

But I heard him in the same way you wake up in the middle of the night and you can't get back to sleep, and you suddenly realize that God is asking you to pray for one of your children. The car became Mount Sinai. The presence of God's spirit was so real that I had to pull off the side of the road. Once the car slowed to a stop, I shut off the ignition and started singing:

To God be the glory
  Great things he hath done.
So loved He the world
  That he gave us His Son.

I sang the songs we used to sing in the Ford Ranch Wagon in Japan:

My Lord knows the way through the wilderness,
And all I have to do is follow.

I sang the songs with motions:

Rolled away, rolled away, rolled away,

156

Every burden of my heart rolled away.

The sun was starting to come up behind me, casting the horizon in the rich blue of a cloudless morning and I sang on:

I've got a home in glory land that outshines the sun,
Way beyond the blue.

When I was a youngster at Warner Elementary School, Uncle Fran the Bible Man used to visit once a month and put on a little program for the whole school. Warner Elementary was a public school, but no one seemed to think it unconstitutional to have a fundamentalist minister stop by the school regularly to talk to kids about Jesus. One time he asked a kid to come up front and sit on a chair he had placed next to the podium. The boy did as he was told, and then Uncle Fran turned to the rest of us and said, "See, that's what faith is. Billy didn't know that the chair would not collapse, but he sat on it anyway."

I loved Uncle Fran, but I thought that was a lousy illustration. Everyone in the all-purpose room *knew* that chair would hold. To me, faith is better illustrated by a chair that looks like it's about to collapse and someone sits in it anyway.

And it holds.

That night along Highway 401, my chair was falling apart. Everything I had been taught in church seemed to be unraveling, but there was only one chair to turn to. It was the one that was held together with the white paste and Scene-o-felts of Sunday school. The one that caused white-gloved ladies to whisper, "We don't run in church." The one that Uncle Gene sat on when he told us about sex and being sanctified. The one I ran past to jump into Lyle Martin's arms.

It did not make sense to turn to God, because in my finite way of looking at things, he had let me down. Not just that night but many times. He had embarrassed me when I tried to witness for him at the beach. He made a fool out of me when I prayed for Sherry Hudberg to be healed. He scared me when Olive Woolsey whooped in church. He ruined my Sundays and kept me from being able to dance or play cards. And now he let me walk into a trap that left me scared, confused, and angry.

Would you sit down in a chair like that?

You would if you had spent a lifetime in church, for whatever oddness there was about the way most of us Baby Boomers were raised in the faith, there was also an unmistakable assurance that when it really counted—when you really came to the end of your rope, God would be there. It was the punch line of every sermon, the theme of every story, the object of every lesson. Whether you denied him three times or doubted him until he showed you his wounds or hung beside him on Calvary, he was there. Whether you backslid or were out of fellowship, he was there. Whether you went forward or carried your guilt around for another day, he was always there. And even if you cursed him for the misfortune that came your way—most likely through your own actions—he refused to be chased away by your anger.

I did not learn all of that on Highway 401 but in the almost two decades of church that I was forced to attend. Every sermon, every altar call, every Sunday school lesson, every love feast, every chorus of every hymn, every busybody who helped my mamma raise me pointed me toward the only thing worthy of being called Savior. When it came time to see if all that I had been taught really worked, I sat in the rickety old chair, and it held me. It was the only sign I needed to get back home.

One of the songs my mom played on our hi-fi on Sunday mornings was a duet by Bill Pierce and Dick Anthony. It was called "I Believe in Miracles," and the only line I remember from it is "I believe in miracles, I've seen a soul set free." I really don't have an

answer to why I have never personally witnessed a miraculous healing of a physical malady, but it no longer weakens my faith. Perhaps it sounds trite, but I believe the greatest miracle God can
perform is to transform the heart of one of his children. There was
no other way to describe me that night than lost. I had been shown
the way but chose to leave it. I don't blame the church for its imperfections or even myself for letting them push me away from my
spiritual heritage. Calvary and Highway 401 intersected that night,
allowing everything I had been taught from a lifetime in church to
make sense.

It took a miracle to hang the stars in place.
It took a miracle to hold the world in place.
    But when he saved my soul,
    Cleansed and made me whole.
It took a miracle of love and grace.

The rest of that miracle is that Audrey went on to marry Glenn,
a wonderful Christian gentleman. For years, the two of them ran a
teen ranch, ministering to troubled young people.

She too had spent a lifetime in church.

13

Discovering Church...Again

*"Halaloo, halaloo,
halaloo, hallelujah!"*

❧

I survived my dark night.

Within the year I met Esther. I was walking through the student center on my way to class when I saw her, and I knew in an instant that she was the one. I did not know her, nor did I speak to her for several weeks and then only briefly.

I just knew.

The end of the school year came, followed by a long summer of factory work. I reported back to campus early to attend a leadership retreat and was surprised to see her in the group waiting to pile into the cars that would take us to the retreat. Since I was driving, I helped organize the caravan, making sure that Esther was assigned to my car but trying not to be too obvious about it. She climbed into the back seat without saying a word, which to me was not a good sign. I wondered how I could convince her that I was the one for *her.*

I shoved a tape into my brand new eight track, and soon a carload of strangers were talking and laughing over the beat of Iron Butterfly. The warm August air blew in through the car's open windows as we sped through miles of southern Michigan farmland. The song was "Inna Gadda Davida," which boasts probably the longest drum solo in rock-and-roll history. The highway was Interstate 69. The wide, green sign indicated the next exit would take us to Coldwater. That's when it happened.

I looked into the rearview mirror, our eyes met, and I knew that *she* knew I was the one for her. We still hadn't said more than a few words to each other, nor would we until later that night. But we both knew.

This time, however, I waited a couple of weeks before I told her I loved her, and I did not feel like the stupidest person on the planet.

We were married in a blizzard about eighteen months after the fateful retreat and were back in church the following Sunday. And we jumped in with a passion. Sunday school teachers. Youth group leaders. We helped plan missionary conventions and Saturday morning men's breakfasts. Since we had both grown up in church, it just seemed natural that church would become a focal point of our lives.

When children came along, we took them to the nursery, just as our parents had taken us, and as they got older we made sure they learned all the songs with motions.

One Sunday, a retired Uncle Dunk was invited back to our church to give the pastoral prayer. Age had not shortened his prayers. Our oldest, Jesse, stood patiently as Uncle Dunk prayed around the world, but it was clear that as the minutes ticked off, Jesse was getting impatient. As Uncle Dunk paused briefly before interceding for yet another mission field, Jesse hollered a distinct and final, "A-men!" and sat down.

In maybe the strangest irony in a life full of them, I returned to Winona Lake where I was given an office upstairs with a big window that gave me a view of the two or three blocks where all of this started. My kids climbed the same trees that guarded the entrance of the Publishing House when I was a boy. They swam in the lake and attended summer services in Billy Sunday Tabernacle. Jesse even slipped out of Sunday school with a few buddies who found their way up into the steeple.

The antenna is gone, and so is the parsonage. It is now full of Sunday school classrooms, which is probably the way it should be. Living in a parsonage is bad enough—no preacher's kid should have to live *inside* the church.

In fact, all of Headquarters is gone—moved to Indianapolis to become more sophisticated and urbane. They bought a warehouse and filled it with offices, and they appear to be running things pretty well, although there is no printing press in the basement.

I left before they moved, knowing it was time to choose my own church. Church was changing, and so was I. A new job in a new town empowered me to do something I had never done before: choose the church my family would attend. It wasn't easy. Four different churches in twelve years may not seem like a lot, but to someone raised in the church, it's outright church-hopping.

If it has been hard for me to find a church to call home—one that I did not fall into by inheritance—I'm not alone. As we were settling into Wheaton, Illinois, in the mid-1980s, I ran into a friend I had known who had lived there quite a while. We were filling our cars with gasoline at a service station, getting caught up on each other's lives. I asked him what church he was attending, hoping to get a lead on a church for our family, and he sort of rolled his eyes.

"Believe it or not, we've been here for seven years, and we still haven't found a church."

This in a town that is home to dozens of well-known Christian ministries with some of the nation's most dynamic evangelical churches. I've heard his story repeated many times by other Boomer friends who tell me that once they finally find a church, it's usually time to move again.

Maybe we were spoiled because we got to sing songs with the motions when we were young, but now, instead of rolling our hands about wildly during "Rolled Away," we've adopted a new set of motions:

Get up. Go to church. Stand for the prayer. Sit for the offering. Listen to the sermon. Stand for the benediction. Walk out. Shake the pastor's hand. Head for the beach.

Regardless of how silly the church of my youth seemed, it always seemed to do something to me. As I sit in church trying to follow the morning praise chorus on the giant video screen, I think often of Olive and all the other saints who were so moved that they couldn't keep quiet. I was always a little embarrassed by them, and still am, and when I visit a church where there is much shouting and waving of arms, I cringe. It seems way overdone and just a bit artificial, though I am sure the hearts of those who do it are right.

Recently I visited a charismatic church and during the singing there was this portly little guy with a beatific smile who swayed in such a manner as to be dancing. I felt like popping him one and telling him to just behave himself, a carnal thought if there ever was one. But what if all that activity is a cry from the child inside who just wants to go back to doing the motions? What if my own stiffness in worship is more of a reaction against excess than a desire to honor God with orderliness and reverence?

We have finally settled in a wonderful church that drives me absolutely crazy with just about everything that makes me uncomfortable: eight microphones on stage, three video screens instead of hymnbooks, the ever-present drum set, casual attire (on Sunday morning!), a shopping-mall foyer where you can buy anything from books to cappuccino to concert tickets (on Sunday!), big hair and jewelry, a Jacuzzi baptismal, and sign-in sheets that are passed down the rows (we are allowed to write in church).

I go because I regularly see the lost get found. When I was a kid, most of the people who got saved had done it several times before. We were a bunch of pretty good people constantly getting saved again. Here, the people who get saved don't even know how to act in church.

A few months ago, it was Phenomenal Family Day at our kids' youth group, meaning that parents were especially invited to join the teenagers for Sunday school, which isn't called Sunday school anymore but something more hip like Power Train or Lighthouse or something. The songs we sang did not resemble "Rolled Away," except that, for some of them, there were motions.

At first, like all good Boomer parents, we just stood politely and sang along. Many of us remember how things can go weird real fast in church and have developed defenses against such silliness. Of course, it felt awkward to stand absolutely rigid while our kids and their leaders waved their arms around and had a good time, but then no one wanted to start doing motions unless another parent did—and we wonder why our kids struggle so with peer pressure. Eventually the youth leader shamed us into joining our teenagers to do the motions on one of the songs, and we sort of got into it.

In my life Lord
Be glorified,
Be glorified.
In my life Lord,
Be glorified today.

I looked across at a girl with pierced eyebrows, nose, ears, tongue, and I don't want to know what else, and saw her smiling and caught a brightness in her eyes that I had not seen before. It spoke of burdens lifted, sins forgiven, and hope. I knew a little of what her young life had already experienced, and it overwhelmed me to see how the power of a song with motions underscored the transformation that apparently had taken place in her life. I looked around and saw other parents with whom I had worshiped politely over the years, and they, like me, were clumsily trying to match the motions with the words. Being white and over forty, we were about a beat-and-a-half behind.

For that briefest of moments, though, we were children back in our Sunday school classrooms, listening to a white-haired lady teaching us to do the motions, and the hidden truths of eternity were revealed to us. Seeing the look on this young girl's face—something we used to call the "shakina glory"—reminded me of what I have missed in most of my grown-up church experience: transcendence—a sense of the supernatural.

Church was boring to seven-year-olds forty years ago, but what I remember most from all those services was that it was a place to do business with God. He attended regularly, and sometimes upset the order of things. This is not to say you have to shout or wave your arms to get God involved. The Lord himself knows there's plenty of arm-waving in churches today—charismatic and non-charismatic—that's pretty much, well, arm-waving. And I don't want to imply that church in the "good old days" was better than church today. It wasn't. My church today has better sermons, better music, better seats (or at least softer), better acoustics, better everything. It's just that despite our lack of sophistication a few decades ago—or maybe because of it—you left church just a little different than when you walked in. You could count on something happening that said, "He's here."

Recently, our church had a guest speaker. I can't remember his name, nor can I remember much of what he said except that he said it in a manner that reminded me of church when I was a kid. He yelled a lot. He told stories that were entertaining but had just enough incredulity that you wondered if they really happened. He pulled all the stops and pushed the right buttons, and I could feel something quicken inside of me—the same feeling I used to feel at revival meetings (and that some of my Reformed friends say is no more than the goose bumps we feel at a Fourth of July parade). When he asked us to come and stand at the altar if we were truly serious about being spiritual leaders in our homes, I could not resist "going forward."

Our teenagers were on the stage with him in a youth choir, and he turned and asked those kids to go find their parents if they had any business to take care of. I was at an angle where I couldn't see my son, and I wondered if he would have the courage to step out in front of the whole church and come stand by me. I half wanted him to, but my old fears of emotion being used to manipulate led me to also hope he didn't get caught up in it.

As I was trying to peek unobtrusively around to see where he was, this fourteen-year-old quarterback blindsided me with a big hug and just held on like he had never done since he was a helpless toddler. He told me that he wanted to be a better Christian, and I told him I wanted to be a better spiritual model for him, and we both forgave each other for the kinds of things a father and son need to forgive each other for.

I did not want to let go of him or that moment.

Maybe the rarity of those moments says more about me than church, but so little of what goes on in church gets through my defenses and into my very being. I have heard people say they don't need church to be close to God; that they are more deeply and profoundly moved by a sunset or a quiet walk in the woods than they have ever been moved in church. I know what they mean and can testify to many similar experiences myself, but it troubles me that I have to watch the sun go down to experience God; that church is often one of the last places where I encounter him so palpably.

I do not blame the church. It has become what we demanded. Comfortable. Professional. Entertaining. Safe. We can invite our friends and not worry about them being embarrassed. We can follow the printed outline of the sermon, nod and note appropriately, and resolve to apply what we have learned to our daily lives. And it makes us better people, which may be part of the problem.

If all church does is make us better people, we might uncomplicate our lives by staying home and reading self-help books.

What stands out in my memory from the church of my childhood—and seems to be happening with regularity in the "minichurches" that our youth groups have become—is a close and powerful encounter with someone bigger than all of us combined. Sometimes it makes us shout. Sometimes it makes us want to dance. Sometimes all we can do is sit transfixed in awe. But we know, we know. The Almighty stopped by.

Glory Land

14

*"I took Jesus as My Savior,
you take him too."*

ॐ

I have been alive for nearly 2,600 Sundays. My best guess is that I have been in church on at least 2,100 of those Sabbaths. If you threw in Wednesday nights and missionary conventions and revival meetings, I have probably been in church for a sermon and some singing on at least 3,000 days. Probably more.

Why?

Believe it or not, I ask myself that question almost fifty-two times a year. And on more occasions than I care to admit, I don't have a ready answer. I have concluded that going to church is an unnatural activity. It does not make sense. For many of us it is the one day of the week when we can sleep in or when we don't have to wear a tie. It would be a perfect time to spend with our always-going-somewhere families. I am not a golfer, but I have to believe this is the absolute most perfect time of the week to hit the links.

Still, we go.

I hate to admit it, but one Sunday during the sermon, I started to list the reasons why, after spending my entire lifetime going to church, I still do it. There were enough good reasons for me to decide to keep going:

Church has kept me married. There have been times when staying married seemed impossible. Aside from our own stubborn wills not to become another statistic, we took our vows in front of some of the very saints who had kept me from running in the sanctuary. In a good way, we see them whenever the bond stretches thin. Their presence in our lives strengthens our resolve to keep the promises we made to each other.

It was in church where we took each of our babies to be dedicated in front of a new batch of saints who would keep them from passing notes. As they mature into adults and worry us with the choices they make—about the faith they either choose or reject— we place our trust in that covenant between the church and our children. How can you walk away from *that?*

The church gave us nurseries and surrogate grammas to hold our babies so that we could enjoy something precious to young couples: an hour away from diapers and colic. It taught each of our kids the motions to "Climb, Climb Up Sunshine Mountain" and their first Bible verse: "Let the little children come to me."

The church made them stars every Christmas in bathrobe dramas in which somehow every child got to say at least one word into the microphone. And it was the church that gave them Sunday school teachers who introduced each of them to Jesus as their Savior. When they went off to college, it was ladies from the church who sent them boxes of cookies with notes of encouragement tucked inside.

When a small tumor sent my wife to an overnight stay in the hospital for surgery shortly after we were married, it was the church that brought me a meal and wrapped us in a "prayer chain." As we awaited the results—two frightened kids barely old enough to vote—it was the church that sent its pastor to reassure us that everything would be all right. He was right.

When that same year Esther's brother, and my friend, was killed in a motorcycle accident, it was the church that cradled our grief, providing a meal for our out-of-town friends and relatives and standing alongside us in the months of loneliness that followed.

When my mother's biopsy revealed a malignancy, it was the church that prayed for her healing. She is still alive!

It was the church that provided us with instant friendships every time we moved, along with pickup trucks and men and boys to move our belongings after the women went through the house with vacuum and mop.

When we took our first camping vacation to Florida and ran directly into Hurricane Agnes, it was the church who opened its arms to a couple too poor to afford a hotel. The parsonage of a church a thousand miles from our home became our home until the waters receded from our flooded campsite.

Church has given me some of the funniest moments of my life. Like the time I volunteered to conduct a service at a local nursing home and preached my little untrained heart out and concluded with a rhetorical question: "Do you still have the joy of your salvation?" To which a voice from the back calmly answered, "No!"

No matter where my job took me, the church was always there. In Lebanon, at the height of the civil war, the church let me worship in one of its holiest temples: a bomb shelter packed with fellow believers whose singing nearly drowned out the artillery fire outside. In Palestine, the church gave me a new family—a Baptist minister who sneaked me into his village so I could eat dinner with other followers of Christ who had lost everything but their faith to the Israeli military. In Cuba, the church taught me that the gates of hell really don't prevail as fifty of us packed into a small living room to sing and pray while sentries kept watch for the police. In Manila, the church introduced me to joyful brothers and sisters who live in a dump known as Smoky Mountain and who wanted to share their only meal of the day with me.

And always, while I was gone, the church became a husband to my wife and a father to my children.

I keep going to church because I need what it gives me. A family. A sense of belonging to something so big it can't be contained. Shoulders to cry on when my kids disappoint me. Shoulders for my kids to cry on when I disappoint them. A holy place where covenants are made.

Going to church gives me a small and imperfect view of heaven, and despite all the silliness that sometimes goes on, I like what I see.

In the church of my youth, Guy Priest pulled the heavy rope that rang the bell calling us all inside to worship. For the twenty or so years I knew him, Guy appeared to be about seventy years old. He was a shy man who seldom spoke, and every summer he would pull a little red wagon up and down the streets of our village selling gladiolas that he grew in his garden. His gait was slowed by a severe limp, yet he would always wave and smile at us kids as we rode past him on our bikes.

As far as I knew, Guy did not have a steady job. In addition to selling stuff from his garden and ringing the church bell, however, he did something else. After every church service he would hobble between the pews, stooping every so often to retrieve a bulletin or Sunday school paper, straighten the hymnals in their racks, and collect a Bible someone left behind. Up and down the rows he would go while everyone else was out in the foyer talking or heading out the door to pot roast and mashed potatoes. If there was a revival meeting or missionary convention, he'd be there every night of the week and always twice on Sundays.

I never really knew Guy, though I know he spoke occasionally with my father. And despite the fact that he lived across the street from us for a few years, I don't ever recall talking to him, except for one time when I was a sophomore in high school.

After a Sunday evening service I was about to walk home when I realized I was missing my Bible. Thinking I had left it at my seat, I slipped back into the sanctuary to find it. As usual, the place was empty except for Guy Priest, who turned around and greeted me just as I walked in. Then he limped over to the end of another pew and picked up my Bible.

"Thanks, Mr. Priest," I said as I took the Bible from his hand. And then, feeling a little awkward about the fact that these were about the only words I'd ever spoken to him in all the time I'd known him, I thought of a question. "Mr. Priest, why do you always stay after church and clean it up?"

I've never forgotten his answer.

"Oh, I guess I just like getting the church ready."

To him, the sanctuary was a holy place where people got real serious with God. It was a tabernacle of praise on Sunday mornings when ordinary people from all walks of life lifted their voices to sing about a mighty fortress and love divine. It was a hospital for the sin-sick and a way station for the weary. It was a lighthouse for the lost and a pillar of fire for the faithful. He had seen teenagers get saved and babies dedicated and missionaries commissioned there.

He rang the bell. He picked up bulletins. He straightened the hymnals. Is there a better job on this planet?

Guy Priest would have had a hard time reading the nineteenth chapter of Revelation, let alone explaining it to a high school sophomore. But watching him get the church ready taught me why I've spent a lifetime in church.

We're getting ready for the wedding.

Every sermon, every Sunday school lesson, every hymn, helped get us ready to meet the Bridegroom. From the glorious anthem on an Easter Sunday to the embarrassment of having to miss a football game because it conflicted with church, I was preparing for that moment when our Lord opens his arms wide and calls me by name and says those words he has waited all his life to say to me.

"Welcome Home."

I have not seen Guy since I left Spring Arbor in 1980. I do not know if he is still living. But someday I will see him. Something tells me he will have found a bell to ring.

I will see Audrey again too. As our families have done before, we will laugh about the time I visited her in Toronto. She will tell me about her boys, and Esther and I will update her about our kids. I will surely introduce her to Lyle Martin, and I know her husband will get along great with Uncle Gene. Maybe we'll throw a party. If my house isn't big enough, we'll head up the street to Sherry Hudberg's place. What an eye she has for decorating. My dad will probably jog by with Uncle Dunk.

Of course, I will have to stop by the Taylors just to say thanks. Jake De Shazer will be there and will probably say something like, "Isn't it fun preaching the gospel here?" Marv and Eleanor Jopling will have coffee waiting for me when I stop by to see their grandchildren. Mrs. Munn will be smoothing out another story on her Scene-o-felt and marvel at the way the flannel never drops off the easel.

Jingo-san loves a party and will probably bring about a million of his friends by to celebrate. Fine with me. For once, we'll have plenty of room in our home.

Grampa Gates will be flipping buttermilk pancakes, while Gramma Cryderman will be asking her son why he isn't wearing his leg brace.

I hope I run into Hako-chan. And Uncle Bob. Maybe Bill will pull out the accordion and Dale the guitar. If they do, Rik and I might try on our kimonos and sing.

We will sing and dance and laugh and play when we get home.

Way beyond the blue.

We want to hear from you. Please send your comments about this book to us in care of the address below. Thank you.

ZondervanPublishingHouse
Grand Rapids, Michigan 49530
http://www.zondervan.com